ERS

**What We
Know About:**

Reading at the Middle and High School Levels:

Building Active Readers
Across the Curriculum
Third Edition

Educational Research Service

Because research and information make the difference.

Educational Research Service
1001 North Fairfax Street, Suite 500, Alexandria, VA 22314
Tel: (703) 243-2100 or (800) 791-9308
Fax: (703) 243-1985 or (800) 791-9309
Email: ers@ers.org • Web site: www.ers.org

Educational Research Service is the nonprofit foundation serving the research and information needs of the nation's K-12 education leaders and the public. Founded by seven national school management associations, ERS provides quality, objective research and information that enable local school district administrators to make the most effective school decisions, both in terms of day-to-day operations and long-range planning. Refer to the last page of this publication to learn how you can benefit from the services and resources available through an annual ERS Subscription.

ERS offers a number of research-based resources that particularly complement this report on the teaching of reading. Please refer to the Order Form at the back of this publication for a listing of some of these materials. Alternatively, visit us online at www.ers.org for a more complete overview of the wealth of K-12 research and information products and services available through ERS.

ERS Founding Organizations:

American Association of School Administrators
American Association of School Personnel Administrators
Association of School Business Officials International
Council of Chief State School Officers
National Association of Elementary School Principals
National Association of Secondary School Principals
National School Public Relations Association

Ordering information: Additional copies of *Reading at the Middle and High School Levels: Building Active Readers Across the Curriculum (Third Edition)* may be purchased at the base price of $20.00 each (ERS School District subscriber price: $10.00; ERS Individual subscriber price: $15.00). Quantity discounts available. Stock No. 0536. ISBN 1-931762-36-8.

Order from: Educational Research Service, 1001 North Fairfax Street, Suite 500, Alexandria, VA 22314. Telephone: (800) 791-9308. Fax: (800) 791-9309. Email: msic@ers.org. Web site: www.ers.org. Add the greater of $4.50 or 10% of total purchase price for postage and handling. Phone orders accepted with Visa, MasterCard, or American Express.

ERS Management Staff:

John M. Forsyth, Ph.D., President and Director of Research
Katherine A. Behrens, Chief Marketing and Business Officer

About the author

Elizabeth A. Wilson has written other publications in the *ERS What We Know About* series including *Effective Early Reading Instruction, Classroom Management to Encourage Motivation and Responsibility*, and the first two editions of *Reading at the Middle and High School Levels*. She has a master's of education in reading and literacy from Bank Street College and currently teaches in a Washington, D.C., area school.

Note: The views expressed in *Reading at the Middle and High School Levels: Building Active Readers Across the Curriculum (Third Edition)* are those of the author and do not necessarily reflect the official positions of Educational Research Service or its founding organizations.

Contents

Foreword

Educational Research Service is pleased to publish this third edition of *Reading at the Middle and High School Levels: Building Active Readers Across the Curriculum.* The popularity of the first two editions and the continuing high level of requests for information on the topic made to ERS's Member Services Information Center make it clear the topic is very important to principals and teachers as well as to reading specialists.

Educators who work with middle and high school students know reading-related issues are critical during a student's secondary school education, with new concerns added as students progress through the grades. Teachers ask: How can I help my students meet standards if they cannot read well enough to comprehend content-area texts? What can I do if some of my students have difficulty reading the assigned text? With all the content that must be covered in the courses I teach, how can I effectively integrate reading instruction into my classes?

Reading at the Middle and High School Levels: Building Active Readers Across the Curriculum addresses these questions and more. This third edition incorporates relevant research since 1999 and expands several of the chapters. In addition, two entirely new chapters—"Phonics versus Literature Immersion: What Struggling Readers Need" and "Schoolwide Support for Literacy Instruction"—have been added.

As with the first and second editions, the focus of the report is on strategies educators can use to improve student reading skills and enhance interest in reading. Many of these strategies are applicable across the curriculum—not just in English classes, but also in subjects such as science and social studies. In addition, some suggestions are provided for using strategies in specific content-area classrooms or with at-risk readers.

The context for this discussion, as with all the reports in the *ERS What We Know About* series, is provided by research findings, informed opinions contained in the professional literature, and examples from school personnel of "what works." Topics addressed in this publication include: approaches for helping poor readers develop good reading strategies, ways to increase student interest in reading for pleasure, and ways social studies, science, or math teachers might effectively incorporate reading instruction within their subject areas.

Reading at the Middle and High School Levels is written for practitioners— for teachers, school administrators, curriculum specialists, and staff development personnel—who understand reading as a key to success for their students, both during the school years and into adulthood. ERS hopes this publication helps you nurture your students as active readers who are empowered to achieve their full academic potential.

John M. Forsyth, Ph. D.
President and Director of Research

Introduction: The Need for High-Quality Literacy Instruction in Secondary Schools

Reading skills are crucial to the academic achievement of students at the middle and high school levels. Most students master the skill of decoding (turning print into speech sounds) in the early grades, but many students are unprepared for the more advanced, compact texts they encounter in fourth grade and beyond. The importance of adolescent literacy is underscored by the following considerations:

1) Learning in content areas such as mathematics, science, and social studies demands strong reading and writing skills.

2) High-stakes testing programs mandate that all middle and high school students achieve high levels of literacy.

3) Requirements for functional literacy are higher than ever before, as our society becomes increasingly information based.

4) Students often lose interest in reading as they get older.

5) Many secondary students lack strategic reading skills, and some are at risk of reading failure. These students require reading instruction targeted to their needs.

6) Secondary teachers have limited time for implementing reading strategies, unless such strategies can be incorporated into approaches for teaching the curriculum.

The National Assessment Governing Board talks about the need for reading instruction to develop readers who:

- read with enough fluency to focus on the meaning of what they read;

- form an understanding of what they read and extend, elaborate, and critically judge its meaning;

- use various strategies to aid their understanding and plan, manage, and check the meaning of what they read;

- apply what they already know to understand what they read;

- can read various texts for different purposes; and

- possess positive reading habits and attitudes (2002, 6).

Issues Concerning Reading in the Content Areas

By the time students reach middle school and high school, they are expected to have the comprehension skills necessary to read in the content areas. Reading in a content area poses new challenges to the secondary student; whereas elementary reading instruction focuses primarily on learning to read, secondary reading instruction focuses on *reading to learn*. That is, reading becomes a tool for gathering information about a subject area. Lyon describes the complex nature of the reading process from the perspective of comprehension:

> In general, if children can read the words on a page accurately and fluently, they will be able to construct meaning at two levels. At the first level, literal understanding is achieved. However, constructing meaning requires far more than literal comprehension. Children must eventually guide themselves through text by asking questions such as: "Why am I reading this, and how does this information relate to my reasons for doing so?" "What is the author's point of view?" "Do I understand what the author is saying and why?" "Is the text internally consistent?" It is this second level of comprehension that leads readers to reflective, purposeful understanding. (1998, 4)

"Some adolescents embrace reading. They engage in it willingly, and they can easily cite favorite authors and works. Other teens seem to find little value in reading. They encounter few difficulties when asked to do it, but they rarely choose to read on a voluntary basis. For still others, reading is a constant struggle. Their inability to deal with print in their everyday lives frustrates them, and they often see little hope in their ability to ever gain much facility to do so" (Curtis 2002, online).

In addition, the reading material required of middle school and high school students becomes more difficult. Gone are the short stories filled with vivid characters and familiar topics that were the basis of the elementary reading program. At the secondary level, textbooks predominate—materials that often are compactly written and contain specialized vocabulary. Students also must learn to read the maps, graphs, charts, and tables that are scattered throughout their texts. Because of these demands on reading skills, secondary students with poor literacy skills are at risk in many of their subject-area courses and so may be more likely to drop out of school. In recent years, researchers have found that direct instruction in reading strategies contributes to student success. Such strategies will be described in Section Five.

One concern content-area teachers often express is how to increase student engagement with the subject. Often, students bring little interest to content classes and are simply there to fulfill basic course requirements. These students may have the skills necessary to read in the content areas, but their lack of interest reduces the amount they learn. The typical structure of a content-area class—centered around a compactly written textbook filled with concepts unfamiliar to the students—only serves to worsen the situation. In such cases, strategies are required that can more actively engage students in their content-area reading materials.

Understandably, content-area teachers want to devote their instructional time to teaching the important concepts of their subject areas. However, placing exclusive emphasis on this task may lead teachers to devalue the importance of teaching reading skills. Because some content-area teachers believe all their students should read on grade level, they do not view reading instruction as their responsibility—despite the reality that not all students come to their classrooms with good reading skills.

NAEP Reading Achievement Levels for Eighth-Grade Students

Advanced

Eighth-grade students performing at the Advanced level should be able to describe the more abstract themes and ideas of the overall text.

For example, when reading **literary** text, Advanced-level eighth graders should be able to make complex, abstract summaries and theme statements. They should be able to describe the interactions of various literary elements (i.e., setting, plot, characters, and theme) and explain how the use of literary devices affects both the meaning of the text and their response to the author's style. They should be able to critically analyze and evaluate the composition of the text.

When reading **informational** text, they should be able to analyze the author's purpose and point of view. They should be able to use cultural and historical background information to develop perspectives on the text and be able to apply text information to broad issues and world situations.

When reading **practical** text, Advanced-level students should be able to synthesize information that will guide their performance, apply text information to new situations, and critique the usefulness of the form and content.

Proficient

Eighth-grade students performing at the Proficient level should be able to show an overall understanding of the text, including inferential as well as literal information.

For example, when reading **literary** text, students at the Proficient level should be able to give details and examples to support themes that they identify. They should be able to use implied as well as explicit information in

articulating themes; to interpret the actions, behaviors, and motives of characters; and to identify the use of literary devices such as personification and foreshadowing.

When reading **informational** text, they should be able to summarize the text using explicit and implied information and support conclusions with inferences based on the text.

When reading **practical** text, Proficient-level students should be able to describe its purpose and support their views with examples and details. They should be able to judge the importance of certain steps and procedures.

Basic

Eighth-grade students performing at the Basic level should demonstrate a literal understanding of what they read and be able to make some interpretations.

For example, when reading **literary** text, Basic-level eighth graders should be able to identify themes and make inferences and logical predictions about aspects such as plot and characters.

When reading **informational** text, they should be able to identify the main idea and the author's purpose. They should make inferences and draw conclusions supported by information in the text. They should recognize the relationships among the facts, ideas, events, and concepts of the text (e.g., cause and effect, order).

When reading **practical** text, they should be able to identify the main purpose and make predictions about the relatively obvious outcomes of procedures in the text (Excerpted from National Assessment Governing Board 2002, 29-30).

NAEP Reading Achievement Levels for Twelfth-Grade Students

Advanced

Twelfth-grade students performing at the Advanced level should be able to describe more abstract themes and ideas in the overall text.

For example, when reading **literary** text, Advanced-level twelfth graders should be able to produce complex, abstract summaries and theme statements. They should be able to use cultural, historical, and personal information to develop and explain text perspectives and conclusions. They should be able to evaluate the text, applying knowledge gained from other texts.

When reading **informational** text, they should be able to analyze, synthesize, and evaluate points of view. They should be able to identify the relationship between the author's stance and elements of the text. They should be able to apply text information to new situations and to the process of forming new responses to problems or issues.

When reading **practical** text, Advanced-level twelfth graders should be able to make critical evaluations of the usefulness of the text and apply directions from the text to new situations.

Proficient

Twelfth-grade students performing at the Proficient level should be able to show an overall understanding of the text, which includes inferential as well as literal information.

When reading **literary** text, Proficient-level twelfth graders should be able to integrate their personal experiences with ideas in the text to draw and support conclusions. They should be able to explain the author's use of literary devices such as irony and symbolism.

When reading **informational** text, they should be able to apply text information appropriately to specific situations and integrate their background information with ideas in the text to draw and support conclusions.

When reading **practical** text, they should be able to apply information or directions appropriately. They should be able to use personal experiences to evaluate the usefulness of text information.

Basic

Twelfth-grade students performing at the Basic level should be able to demonstrate an overall understanding and make some interpretations of the text.

For example, when reading **literary** text, Basic-level twelfth graders should be able to explain the theme, support their conclusions with information from the text, and make connections between aspects of the text and their own experiences.

When reading **informational** text, Basic-level twelfth graders should be able to explain the main idea or purpose of a selection and use text information to support a conclusion or make a point. They should be able to make logical connections between the ideas in the text and their own background knowledge.

When reading **practical** text, they should be able to explain its purpose and the significance of specific details or steps (Excerpted from National Assessment Governing Board 2002, 31-32).

Barriers to Focusing on Reading in Content-Area Classrooms

Making time for content-area reading instruction is certainly not an easy task, especially given the time demands already placed on teachers. However, planning ahead to integrate such instruction into the curriculum can help to make content-area reading instruction possible and effective, rather than just an add-on.

Reading specialists can be an important resource for teachers as they make this shift. These specialists should work in cooperation with the content teacher, optimally in the content-area classroom itself—where students are struggling with real reading tasks—rather than in separate lessons about reading (Henwood 2000). Because reading specialists understand the basic reading problems, they can suggest possible solutions to students or teachers, and can work directly with teachers to implement new approaches. Content teachers also will need additional administrative support, especially in cases where reading specialists are not available. Administrative support means developing inservice programs, as well as providing teachers with planning time or time to meet with other teachers. More information about professional development is included in Section Eight.

Evidence suggests it makes a difference when teachers *do* create time for content-area reading instruction. Strategies that teachers found to be effective in improving content-area achievement included: activating background knowledge before reading by brainstorming about the meanings of key vocabulary terms; asking students to keep a journal of content-area concept definitions; and asking students to create their own learning guides, instead of relying on teacher-prepared materials.

High-Stakes Testing

Faced with mounting numbers of state- and districtwide tests, schools—and so teachers—are pressured to cover more content in an effort to have their students meet standards, or otherwise face potential intervention or restructuring. These tests also have forced school districts to confront the problem of a significant number of poor readers at the middle and high school levels. Content-area teachers are justifiably focused on imparting subject-area knowledge, but they also need to be part of the effort to make sure no student is left behind due to poor literacy skills.

The Changing Definition of "Functional Literacy"

Our society's shift from a manufacturing base to a technological base has profound implications for the adolescents in our middle and high schools. Students who come of age in the 21st century will need advanced levels of literacy—they will read and write more than those of any other generation before them (Vacca 2002). They will need strong reading and writing skills to handle the flood of information that is brought on by instantaneous communication and ever-changing Internet sites. The National Assessment Governing Board expands on this:

> In a world driven by information technology, the complexity of reading literacy is increasing as the format of texts becomes more diverse. Varied texts such as CD-ROMs, Web pages, newspapers, and magazines place different demands on the reader. As information technology grows, people will encounter even more varied texts and will be called on to use information in new ways (2002, 7).

Students will need to think critically about the information they read, form their opinions, and respond thoughtfully. When reading unverified Internet sources, students will need to carefully evaluate them for accuracy and authenticity, and use the information effectively.

Students Lose Interest in Reading

At the same time that required reading skills become more challenging, the likelihood that students are reading for pleasure declines. This is an important point, since reading for fun is connected to academic achievement. Donna Ogle, past president of the International Reading Association, sheds some light on this issue:

> Today's students don't choose to read in their independent time very much because there's so much out there for them to do. When students haven't had experience in reading widely, they don't have the wealth of background knowledge that teachers assume they have. And if you don't know much about content, you're also going to struggle in reading because vocabulary is crucial in reading text (in D'Arcangelo 2002, 13).

Research has confirmed the link between reading for fun and reading achievement. U.S. Department of Education reports based on data from the National

Assessment of Educational Progress (NAEP) indicate students who read daily for fun have higher average NAEP reading scores than students who never read for fun (National Center for Education Statistics 2001b).

Although there are alternative explanations for this correlation—either that better readers enjoy reading and so read more, or that reading more actually contributes to reading competency—some combination of these two probably describes the relationship. Moreover, although the impact of leisure reading habits on reading competency would be difficult to isolate, most people—educators, parents, and students themselves—would agree that reading for pleasure should be encouraged.

On a broader scale, although the influential 1985 report *Becoming a Nation of Readers* underscored the importance of leisure reading to reading development, no increase in leisure reading has been observed in the years since this report was released. In fact, the percentage of 17-year-olds who reported reading for fun on a daily basis was lower in 1996 than in 1984, and the percentage who reported never reading for fun was higher. This study indicates there might be a pattern of decreased reading for fun as students age: whereas 54 percent of nine-year-olds reported in 1999 that they read for fun on a daily basis, only 28 percent of 13-year-olds and 25 percent of 17-year-olds reported these leisure reading habits (National Center for Education Statistics 2001c).

Students Lack Critical Reading Skills and Strategies

Policy makers have focused their attention (and funding) on improving reading programs in the early grades. Yet according to international comparisons older students also need of this type of support (Allington 2002).When compared with students from other nations, U.S. fourth-graders rank high in terms of achievement in reading, science, and math. The international rankings for U.S. middle schoolers and high schoolers, however, show a substantial drop from that of fourth-grade levels (National Center for Education Statistics 2001). In addition, the National Assessment of Educational Progress in reading reports no overall change in reading ability from 1992 to 2000 for even the younger students; almost 40 percent of fourth-grade students cannot read at a "basic" level (Salinger 2003).

For some middle and high school students, the problem is so severe that they are at risk of failure in content-area courses due to problems with reading.

NAEP 2003 Reading Results for Eighth-Graders

- The average reading score for eighth-graders decreased by one point between 2002 and 2003; the score in 2003 was higher than that in 1992.

- The percentage of eighth-graders scoring in the four major categories is as follows: *Below Basic*—26 percent; *At Basic*—42 percent; *At Proficient*—29 percent; and *At Advanced*—3 percent.

- The percentage of eighth-grade students performing at or above *Proficient* was higher in 2003 than in 1992.

- The percentage of eighth-grade students performing at or above *Basic* decreased by one point between 2002 and 2003; the percentage was higher in 2003 than in 1992 (National Assessment Governing Board 2003, online).

NAEP 2002 Reading Results for Twelfth-Graders

- The twelfth-grade average score in 2002 was lower than in 1992 and 1998.

- The percentage of twelfth-graders scoring in the four major categories is as follows: *Below Basic*—26 percent; *At Basic*—38 percent; *At Proficient*—31 percent; and *At Advanced*—5 percent.

- At grade 12, declines in performance since 1992 were evident across most of the score distribution (10th, 25th, 50th, and 75th percentiles).

- The percentages of twelfth-graders who performed at or above the *Basic* and *Proficient* levels decreased between 1998 and 2002, and thus fell below levels seen in 1992 (National Assessment Governing Board 2003b, online).

These students are likely to have already experienced failure in school and to have low literacy skills. Such students may have learning disabilities, may just be starting to learn English, or may be merely reluctant readers who have not mastered grade-level reading skills. Demands in the higher grades for content-area reading competency create continuing problems for these students, with reading deficiencies negatively affecting many other areas of school performance.

> A quarter of our country's eighth-graders are reading at "below basic" levels. Not being able to read and comprehend increasingly complex course material is a major factor in a student's decision to leave school early. With a national graduation rate of only 70 percent (a figure that falls to around 50 percent in urban areas), we must recognize and address this correlation. The consequences of not doing so—to the individual and to our nation's economic and social future—cannot be reversed (Excerpt from a letter to President George W. Bush by the Alliance for Excellent Education, December 2003).

Past failures with reading, and with school in general, typically result in low levels of motivation. However, it is with these students—who need to be actively engaged—that the most *un*motivating techniques often are used. Remedial reading courses often are taught at the students' present level of functioning, with emphasis on basic skills rather than on the importance of reading for meaning. Instruction for these students will be discussed in Section Two.

While other students' reading problems may not be as pronounced, they nonetheless present a significant obstacle to content-area learning. High-stakes tests have exposed the reading deficits of many middle and high school students who might otherwise have eked by. According to Vacca (2002), strategic reading skills are what many adolescent readers lack. They appear skillful in reading mechanics but do not engage in higher-level interaction with the text, such as prediction, synthesis, inference, or summarization. Instead, they are simply "going through the motions of reading and writing–saying the words or putting the words on paper" (Vacca 2002, 9). Strategies for helping adolescents develop crucial reading strategies are discussed in Section Five.

Limited Time for Implementing Reading Strategies

In a survey of barriers to content-area teachers' implementation of reading strategy instruction, the most common response was lack of time (Barry 2002). A related issue reported by teachers was pressure to cover content: teachers found that taking time to model strategies limited the amount of material that could be covered. They reported that it takes time not only to instruct students about strategies, but also simply to develop their own in-depth understanding of a strategy that is necessary in order to teach it to students. Another challenge that applies particularly to new teachers is confidence—developing a comfort zone with strategy instruction. Barry writes: "It takes time to feel comfortable enough in a classroom to slow down and allow quiet time to predict, question, summarize, visualize, and think aloud" (2002, 140).

Since pressure to cover content and lack of time are constraints teachers experience when they want to set aside time for teaching reading strategies or activating student interest in reading, teachers must continually make determinations not only about the *effectiveness* of any given strategy, but also about its *efficiency* as well. Any procedure used must be efficient in terms of time and payback. The primary focus should be on strategies that work well—that is, strategies that encourage higher levels of learning for *all* students, while recognizing the particular needs of those students who are most at risk for reading failure. Support from the school's reading specialists is also critical. Unfortunately, secondary schools frequently do not provide this kind of support.

Building Active Readers Across the Curriculum

Given that reading is a critical concern for those dealing with middle level and high school students, what is the major purpose of secondary school reading instruction?

In its position statement on adolescent literacy, the International Reading Association asserts that adolescents entering the "adult world" today will need to perform more reading and writing tasks—and contend with a greater flood of information—than at any other time in human history (International Reading Association 1999). Therefore, the overriding goal behind any reading strategy should be to foster active, engaged, independent readers. In recent years, approaches to reading instruction have focused on the constructive nature of reading. That is, the meaning of a text is not contained within the printed words themselves, but rather arises from the reader's interaction with the text. The reader actually creates meaning by synthesizing the material with his or her background knowledge and personal experience. The strategies described in this book are intended to put readers in an active role, while improving reading skills and increasing motivation to read.

This report addresses reading in the content areas as well as reading in the English classroom, providing a number of strategies that both content teachers and English teachers can use to improve reading skills and enhance interest in reading. Although English can certainly be considered a content area with its own subject matter, the term "content area" will be used in this report to refer only to non-English classes (subjects such as social studies, math, and science). The term is used in this way because opportunities for reading instruction and reading-related activities often can be structured more easily into the English classroom than into other subject areas. Therefore, the kinds of issues English teachers and non-English teachers face regarding reading instruction are, in some cases, quite different. Moreover, the research itself makes this distinction. Yet despite the differences, these two areas also contain similarities, which will become apparent as the topic is addressed.

Section Two

Phonics Versus Literature Immersion: What Struggling Readers Need

Over the last decade, disappointing national scores on the reading portion of the National Assessment of Educational Progress (NAEP) sometimes have been attributed to insufficient attention to phonics-related skills. As a result, remedial reading instruction has been adjusted in many schools to increase the emphasis on phonics instruction (Vaughn, Klinger, and Bryant 2001). Although phonemic awareness and phonics-related skills are undoubtedly significant components of reading acquisition, many educators and researchers question the value of emphasizing these components with all struggling adolescent readers. Adolescent reading problems are more likely to be comprehension-based; only a minority of struggling older readers have decoding difficulties (Association for Supervision and Curriculum Development 2000; Greenleaf, Jimenez, and Roller 2002; Salinger 2003; Vaughn, Klinger, and Bryant 2001). In fact, focusing primarily on decoding skills may be detrimental to these readers, as Jimenez explains (in Greenleaf, Jimenez, and Roller 2002):

> In my work with intermediate-level and middle school Latino/Latina students, I found relatively few students who could benefit from intensive code instruction. Some of them did need help in this area; most of them did not. They needed help with fluency, and they needed help with purpose. The majority had suffered for years from code-emphasis instruction, and as a result they found reading a completely meaningless activity (488).

In the same article, Greenleaf, Jimenez, and Roller expand on Jimenez' point, discussing the long-term implications for struggling readers:

> Phonics is seldom the limiting factor for adolescent readers. Limited views of their capabilities, limited opportunities to draw on their lived knowledge and experience, and limited opportunities to learn and practice higher level literacies and crack the code of academic texts

have historically been factors that . . . systematically exclude many students from literate practices that end up being gatekeeping practices in school (489).

Factors Necessary for Students to Become Proficient Readers

In their review of research on middle and high school students who are struggling readers, Peterson et al. identify four factors key to increasing students' proficiency:

(a) the motivation to read, (b) the ability to decode print, (c) the ability to comprehend language, and (d) the ability to transact with text (i.e., to actively seek information and make personal responses) (2000, 14).

Collins talks about the "cycle of failure" in which many low-performing middle and high school readers are caught. Thus, in addition to helping these students build skills, "building their confidence is essential" (1996, online).

The effectiveness of literature-based activities with struggling readers has been demonstrated by research. For example, a reading workshop with elements such as self-selected texts and journal responses was found to improve the reading skills of at-risk high schoolers (Kletzien and Hushion 1992). Also, one case study of struggling adolescent readers who participated in a year-long reading workshop found 19 out of 22 students showed improved scores on a standardized reading test (Williams 2001). The author writes:

The biggest benefits come when struggling readers see themselves as readers. At the end of the year I ask students to take out their reading record sheets that they have used to keep a record of all the books they have read and abandoned. As they count how many books they have read or heard since the beginning of the year, it is not unusual for me to hear comments similar to the one made by a sixth grader, "I can't believe I read this many books. This is the most books I have ever read." For the first time these students begin to feel that they belong to the reading community. Reading becomes something they can and want to do (601).

Components of a Literature-Based Approach for Struggling Readers

A literature-based reading workshop might include high-interest reading materials, opportunities to discuss reading materials in small groups, or student dramatization of plays. Many such approaches are described in Section Four. One particularly critical element is sustained silent reading, which increases automaticity, fluency, vocabulary, and background knowledge (Greenwood 2002; Hirsch 2003). Whittier and Blokker (2001) recommend that struggling readers engage in sustained silent reading for at least 200 minutes per week, using appropriate texts that can be read with 95 percent accuracy. For more information about silent reading, see Section Four.

In addition, struggling readers need instruction that builds on their own literacy experiences. For example, within Hispanic culture letter writing is an important form of literacy for sustaining community; also Latino/Latina students regularly carry out translations on behalf of their families (Greenleaf, Jimenez, and Roller 2002). To invite these literacy experiences into the classroom, teachers must first learn about these experiences—from the students and their communities, or from research. Some ways to invite student literacy experiences into the classroom include:

- having students tell or write personal reading histories in which they reflect on and share their reading journeys in and outside of school; and

- asking students to bring in their out-of-school reading material (with parameters to avoid objectionable texts), which they can then share with the class. Teachers, in turn, can use the texts for think-alouds in which they demonstrate reading strategies (Greenleaf, Jimenez, and Roller 2002).

Instruction for Students with Decoding Difficulties

The fact remains, however, that a minority of adolescent students do have serious difficulty with decoding. These students need intensive, systematic phonics-based approaches that are woven into a literature-rich curriculum—but that are not the sole focus of remediation efforts. One language curriculum—the LANGUAGE! Program—combines these approaches. During six months of enrollment in program, participants averaged gains of about three years in different literacy areas (including word recognition and comprehension) (Greene 1998).

Here are some phonics-based approaches that may be helpful to students when part of a balanced literacy program:

- Focus on meaningful chunks of letters within words. Salinger writes "instruction that focuses on identifying syllables as important clues to word meaning gives students a valuable tool for decoding unfamiliar words" (2003, 82). The benefits of this approach were highlighted by a Canadian study that found a decoding-by-analogy program (involving word chunks) improved the reading scores of poor readers at the high school level. After three to four months of instruction in the Glass Analysis technique, these readers exhibited an increase in mean reading grade equivalent of approximately three grades (Penney 2002).

- Instead of asking students to passively break apart multisyllabic words, ask them to use root words to construct new words—just as younger students play with phonemes to make up rhymes (Salinger 2003).

- Reinforce rhyming skills by asking students to read poetry and song lyrics, and even create their own. Encourage students to rhyme multisyllable words (Brucker and Piazza 2002).

- Invite students to analyze poems with strong alliteration, and then write poems in this manner (Brucker and Piazza 2002).

- Help students learn to pay close attention to small differences between words (such as pacific/specific, scalding/scolding). This focuses their attention on speech sounds, helps them link speech sounds to letters, and can increase their vocabularies (Salinger 2003).

- Similarly, use word links to manipulate sounds within words. A word link is a series of words that are linked because only one or two phonemes change from one word to the next (for example, pickle, fickle, tickle, tackle, tackled, spackled, etc.). Observing students read through this list can provide information about reading skills and error patterns. Students can also create their own word link lists (Brucker and Piazza 2002).

Section Three

Motivational Factors Related to Reading

Reading achievement is not just a matter of reading ability; it also can be significantly affected by how students feel about the activity of reading and about themselves as readers. The roles that factors such as student attitude toward reading and student interest in reading play are of increasing interest to researchers and practitioners. Motivational factors play an important role in reading habits, preferences, and achievement level, and thus should be a consideration when planning reading instruction. Four major motivational factors will be discussed: developmental needs during adolescence, attitude toward reading, interest in reading, and factors such as television viewing and family practices.

Adolescent Developmental Needs

By examining some of the developmental needs that characterize adolescence, researchers have identified issues critical to developing responsive, effective secondary reading instruction. Adolescents need opportunities for:

- *Self-exploration and definition.* Adolescents need to explore their new cognitive and linguistic abilities, and to consider how they might use them in their future adult roles. Providing free reading periods in which students choose their reading, as well as having students write personal responses to text in dialogue journals, are good ways to facilitate self-exploration.

- *Competence and achievement.* Adolescents often feel unsure of themselves. Assessment of literacy achievement, therefore, should focus on providing information on student progress, rather than simply judging academic successes and failures.

- *Diversity.* Teenagers vary greatly in their interests and abilities. Teachers should allow not only for diversity in reading material, but also for different types of class activities, ranging from quiet, independent work to social interaction in literature discussion groups.

- *Physical activity.* Adolescents tend to need more physical activity than is provided in the typical intermediate or secondary level classroom. A workshop-like setting that includes literacy activities ranging from individual writing to paired or small-group work and large-group discussion, in addition to teacher lectures, can provide opportunities for movement and activity (Davidson and Koppenhaver 1993).

One middle school teacher describes how she took advantage of adolescents' distinct developmental needs to get them involved with literature:

> How do adults help thirteen- and fourteen-year-olds harness their energy, sublimating all those new and arresting drives so that they can be still long enough to learn? Although no secret formulas exist, I tried to use the qualities—being provocative, challenging authority, finding their own individuality, seeking justice, and believing in their own immortality—that set eighth graders apart as a way to hook them on to language learning. I chose to tap rather than to fight those peculiar tendencies. I tried to capitalize on eighth graders' desire to be in charge of their lives. By design I connected the special projects we did, the formal debates we had, and the literature we read with the temperament of rapidly changing adolescents (Krogness 1995, 49-50).

This teacher selects texts that grapple with themes central to adolescence. Such themes abound in young adult books, such as the theme of disobeying authority in Robert Cormier's *The Chocolate War*. Although young adult books are often viewed as light reading materials that are not of the literary quality of the "classics," they allow adolescents to bridge the gap between childhood reading materials and the classics. Young adult literature in the classroom will be discussed in more detail in Section Four.

Attitude toward Reading

There is a strong relationship between reading attitude and reading comprehension. For example, O'Sullivan (1992) examined what she termed "students' motivational beliefs about their reading ability"—beliefs that they

"It was the summer of 1989, and I moved slowly in the porch swing, taking advantage of the Kentucky twilight to choose a new novel for my reluctant eighth graders to read that fall. 'You can do it,' was my constant comment to these students. 'You can do it,' I'd say when they would reluctantly open a book and then just stare at the pages.... Motivating reluctance was sometimes wearying work.... One book, *Hatchet*, kept rising to the top of the pile, where I would push it aside and try to ignore it.... Finally, I opened the cover, and what I discovered transformed my teaching.

Hatchet exploded all over my classroom that fall. Ninety eighth graders read every word of the book, and, like me, they were hooked from the moment the pilot died on page eleven. I'd ordered a classroom set of books, and every single student was reading as if inspired. It was astonishing. Truthfully, I was leaping out of bed in the mornings, eager to get to school. My students simply could not get enough of the story about thirteen-year-old Brian crashing alone in the Canadian wilderness and surviving for fifty-four days. For the most part, these readers were grappling with their own efforts to survive adolescence, to thrive in their rural Eastern Kentucky community, and, possibly, like Brian, to understand a parent's divorce" (Wood 2001, 67).

could "take control of their reading, set high standards, and achieve their goals." She found that the beliefs of her low-income subjects significantly influenced their reading achievement. Further, these student beliefs were heavily influenced by the beliefs of teachers and parents.

Because of the relationship between reading attitude and reading comprehension, assessing students' attitudes should be a part of any class that includes reading. Ways to assess attitude include:

- *Questionnaires*. This might include such questions as: How do you feel about reading? Do you consider yourself a reader? If not, what don't you like about reading? Do you consider yourself a writer?

- *Reading autobiographies*. Each student writes a personal history of his or her reading experiences.

- *Portfolios*. This consists of a student's responses to individual texts.

- *Letters of intention*. Students write letters to themselves at the beginning of the school year, stating what they hope and expect from the year to come (Krogness 1995).

Personal Interest

There are a variety of ways to find out more about the individual interests of students. For example, students can fill out interest inventories—questionnaires or checklists that make the teacher aware of common interests among students. The teacher can then assign reading materials that involve these shared interests or use a struggling student's personal interests as a way to tap motivation. If thematic units are part of the curriculum, the inventories can be used as sources for topic ideas. Or, students can interview each other about their interests and report them to the teacher.

Teachers also should keep abreast of general teen reading interests; lists of teenagers' favorite books are readily available. As an example, Young Adult's Choices is published every year by the International Reading Association in the *Journal of Adolescent and Adult Literacy* (access online at http://www.reading.org/choices/). Each year 30 titles are chosen by approximately 4,500 students in grades 7-12 from different regions of the United States. Books are selected from new publications donated by North American publishers.

External Influences

Environmental factors such as television and parental role modeling can exert a powerful motivational influence as well. While these factors may seem to be minimally within the control of the school environment, there are several effective ways educators can address them, such as encouraging students to be informed and critical television watchers, and promoting parental involvement in school.

Parental Involvement

Younger students who read for fun typically have parents who model reading. However, surveys of adolescents reveal important additional findings about this relationship. Studies of 13- and 17-year-olds' reading practices found that those students who reported infrequent reading activities in their home had lower reading proficiencies. The same study found that students with higher reading proficiencies had more books in the home and more home literacy resources such as dictionaries, atlases, and computers (National Center for Education Statistics 1996).

Suggested ways to get parents involved include:

- *Project Bookshelf:* Post announcements in school bulletins and newspaper press releases, encouraging parents to go through their bookshelves and look for appealing books to donate to classroom libraries.

- *Parent tutors:* Recruit parents to tutor reading skills. Parents may be volunteers, or they might be paid through grant funds. They should be provided with training about the school's reading program and about techniques for teaching reading.

- *Reading advisory board:* Create a board composed of teachers and parents to explore how teachers and parents can work together to improve the reading program.

- *Reading awareness week:* The week might include activities such as visits from local authors, including parent authors. Teachers can send home lists of recommended books, tips on selecting books for adolescents, or bookmarks.

- *Book discussion groups:* Invite parents to come to the classroom and participate in book talks with students.

- *Family literacy programs:* Family literacy programs are designed to work with parents and their children (typically at the preschool level or in the early grades) for the purpose of improving the literacy development of the children or the entire family. Generally, adolescents are included in family literacy programs only when they are the parents; however, these programs might also be beneficial for at-risk adolescent students from families with low literacy skills. Programs might include parent literacy education, support groups for parents, or opportunities for planned interactions between parents and children (Morrow, Tracey, and Maxwell 1995).

The Effects of Television

One common concern among educators, parents, and others is that television has a negative impact on students' academic achievement, especially their reading skills. When children spend time watching television, that activity is replacing other activities such as homework and reading. In addition, watching television promotes passivity because it does not require much mental effort and may reduce a child's ability to concentrate.

When weighing the potentially harmful effects of television, one issue to consider is the amount of time spent per day on this activity. Analyses of NAEP data found that, at all three grade levels tested (four, eight, and 12), students who reported watching three or fewer hours of television a day had higher average NAEP reading scores than their peers who reported watching four or more hours a day (National Center for Education Statistics 2001b).

In a more positive light, television has been used successfully in secondary classrooms as a powerful teaching tool (Lawrence et al. 1993). Used appropriately, instruction using television capitalizes on the strong interest many adolescents have in this medium and also provides an opportunity to think critically about subtle messages embedded in programs. Examples of projects include: studying the propaganda techniques used in advertising; evaluating the quality of television journalism (especially in light of the amount of "tabloid" programs shown every day); and analyzing PBS programming.

Hibbing and Rankin-Erickson make another suggestion for turning students' familiarity with television into a resource. They talk about using the analogy of a "television in the mind . . . [to help] students realize that there should be more going on in the reading process than just 'barking the words'" (2003, 760). They expand on this approach:

> We talk about the television screen that we "watch" as we read, and we use think-alouds to talk about the pictures on our mental screen as we read. We emphasize the need for pictures to match the words. We explain that when the pictures and words do not match (e.g., a student's mind wanders to picturing the dance on Friday night rather than picturing the actions of the text), it is as if the channel has been switched from the "story" channel to the "dance" channel. We teach students they need to do something when this "channel switching" happens, such as refocus or reread in order to get back on the right channel" and create an appropriate mind picture (2003, 760).

Approaches for Actively Engaging Students in Reading

In his review of research on instructional strategies that provide the most support for student learning in the language arts, Squire highlights the:

> positive connection between extensive reading and improved reading comprehension. [In addition], providing opportunities for students to discuss what they have read—to become active participants in making meaning from written text—has also been proven to help students' reading skills to grow (2004, 127).

Educators' every-day experiences support these research-based findings and, in response, some curriculum reform efforts have focused on the need to actively engage students in learning. Hallmarks of an interactive reading program include:

- an important role for students in suggesting or selecting reading materials;

- time set aside during the school day for students to read silently or aloud;

- an abundance of print materials in the classroom;

- opportunities for students to respond to reading material (such as literature, newspaper articles, and biographies) in writing—for example, by writing in dialogue journals;

- time for students to discuss their reading materials in small groups; and

- opportunities for students to draw on personal experience in order to understand what they are reading.

These are all components of the whole-language approach to reading instruction. The whole-language approach emphasizes the importance of natural learning situations in which language is dealt with in context, and in which meaning-making is considered the central focus of reading and writing (McWhirter 1990). It is considered especially important that students read and write about things that interest them. Because natural learning situations are central to this theory, whole-language research relies more on naturalistic observations, such as case studies, than on quantitative evaluations (Goodman 1992).

Although the whole-language approach is usually discussed in the context of the elementary grades, a study of two teachers and four English classes reveals the advantages of implementing an interactive approach to reading at the secondary level. After the teachers were given guidance about interactive reading methods, they modified their teaching styles and established small groups for literature discussion, assigned students to write joint essays on literary topics of their own choosing, and incorporated student suggestions into lesson plans. Teachers reported that they had revitalized themselves and their classrooms; students read more and expressed more interest in what they read (Gross 1991).

Encouraging Students to Read More and Read Widely

The more students read, the better they read. What type of environment creates a classroom that turns students on to reading? Key factors include: providing choice in reading materials, establishing a print-rich environment, including light reading and young adult literature in the curriculum, exposing students to a wide variety of materials, making time for in-school free reading, reading aloud, and designing thematic units. This section will take a look at factors that can increase reading activity and, subsequently, the enjoyment of reading.

Choice in Reading Materials

Results from a study by Kellerman emphasize the mismatch often found between books students prefer and those that are assigned: "Only four out of the fifteen books chosen by teachers for free reading assignments matched the students' top six preferences in terms of interest [areas]. The remainder of the books were among the students' least preferred types of books" (1991, 14-15). Moreover, case study research clearly indicates students prefer being able to select their own reading (Gross 1992; Kletzien and Hushion 1992).

Instead of requiring the entire class to read a particular book, teachers can provide students with a list of books from which students choose the titles that most appeal to them. It is critical that this list be designed with student interests in mind. Providing students with choice, however, does not mean the teacher leaves students on their own—many students are likely to need guidance and advice during their selection process. In one study, a high school teacher hypothesized that students' reluctance to read was due to their lack of knowledge about how to choose books. To address this issue, she asked her students to practice creating book previews in the computer lab, and then share their previews with one another. She found that after a few weeks, students reported more enjoyment of reading and a higher perception of their reading abilities. In addition, more students were reading regularly than before (Wright 1998).

Creating a Print-Rich Environment: Classroom and School Libraries

Research also supports the importance of the link between the number of books available to students and the amount of reading they do. However, research indicates that classroom libraries are often designed with insufficient attention to student interests: a study of middle school students' reading preferences and access to reading materials found students had limited school access to their preferred reading materials, such as scary books, comics, and magazines about pop culture. In fact, classrooms ranked a distant last for book sources, even for students from low-income families (Worthy, Moorman, and Turner 1999).

Well-chosen collections representing a range of topics and difficulty levels in classroom libraries or schoolwide library media centers help to get adolescents excited about the world of books. These libraries could be set up in content-area classes as well as English classes and could contain a supply of light reading materials relating to the subject under study. Atwell (1998) contends that not only does a classroom library invite students to browse, chat about books, and be selective about their choices, but it also demonstrates that reading is a high priority to the school.

Classroom library materials also should represent a wide range of reading levels, because struggling readers will improve their skills through opportunities to read materials with 95 percent word recognition accuracy (Ivey 1999). "High/low books" (high interest/low vocabulary materials) are particularly appropriate for struggling adolescent readers; several bibliographies of these materials are available. Picture books that include content relevant to the subject area are also a valuable addition to the classroom library. Such books are appealing to many early adolescents, provide reading practice for struggling readers, can offer a rich cultural diversity of stories and artwork, expose students to advanced vocabulary, and work well as an introduction to abstract topics because they activate background knowledge and stimulate curiosity.

The Young Adult Library Services Association, a division of the American Library Association, annually recommends a list of "Quick Picks for Reluctant Young Readers." The list is "geared to the teenager who, for whatever reason, does not like to read." Available at www.ala.org.

A national study of high school literature programs examined the role of the school library and found good libraries make a difference to the literature program (Applebee 1993). Applebee compared school libraries in award-winning schools—those that had consistently produced winners in the NCTE Achievement Awards in Writing Program—with a random sample of public schools. The study found there are three vital components to a good school library: collection size, accessibility, and title availability.

- *Collection size.* Award-winning schools reported a greater number of volumes available, yet no difference was found in terms of per-pupil statistics. This suggests that *per-pupil calculations may not be as critical as sheer collection size,* as one researcher who reviewed these findings speculates: ". . . this may be a case in which statistics obscure rather than enlighten. Students and teachers don't experience a library on a 'per-pupil' basis. More volumes available is simply that— more volumes in a collection that can be devoted to literature topics proportionately" (Burroughs 1993, 163).

- *Accessibility.* An accessible library is one that has extended hours (perhaps open before and after school, or on weekends), is open to the general public, and contains resource-sharing networks (such as inter-library loan programs). Upon reviewing research on library accessibility, Krashen (1993) concludes that access to school libraries, larger library collections, and longer library hours all result in more reading.

- *Title availability.* Schools in Applebee's survey were asked whether or not their library held 24 specific titles. Included on the list were works of literature by women and minority authors, as well as young adult books. Award-winning schools had more of these titles (19 out of 24) than did the random sample of public schools (13 out of 24).

Young Adult Literature in the Classroom

Adolescents who engage in frequent nonacademic reading out of school (such as learning about a sports hero, or reading a friend's email or lyrics off a CD) may have difficulty reconciling that kind of literate activity with school-required reading. Broadus and Ivey write of adolescent readers:

> . . . their out-of-school reading is driven by their open-ended explorations of personal interests, identities, and social roles, a far cry from the kinds of teacher-driven, product-oriented reading expected of them in school.... In reality, the need for teachers to pay more attention to students' personal interests in school reading may be even more crucial for struggling readers who, through years of nonfluent, unfocused, and failed attempts at school reading, may have never developed real purposes for any kind of reading (2002, 7).

The types of reading that typically appeal to adolescents include teen romances, comics, science fiction, and problem novels (novels with teen characters who have realistic problems, such as dealing with divorce, puberty, or alcohol abuse). These books stand in sharp contrast to the types of literature prescribed in the curriculum of some secondary schools, which may include predominantly such classics as *Hamlet*, *Of Mice and Men*, and *The Scarlet Letter* (Applebee 1993) and exclude works such as Cormier's *I Am the Cheese* and L'Engle's *Ring of Endless Light*. More and more, however, teachers are realizing the value of bringing young adult literature into the classroom, for these books have the potential to spark interest in even the most reluctant readers. One obstacle to incorporating these books into the curriculum is that teachers rarely have complete freedom over the literature they teach. The great majority, however, have at least some leeway to add materials to the core selection or ask to have additional selections approved (Applebee 1993).

Contrary to prevailing beliefs, the term "young adult literature" is not synonymous with low-quality literature. In fact, a few of these works have even managed to establish themselves in the secondary curriculum—for example, *Lord of the Flies* and *The Outsiders* (Applebee 1993). Eighth-grade teacher Nancie Atwell writes:

> The last thirty years have witnessed an explosion in the volume of novels and short stories written expressly for young adults, adolescent literature of breadth, depth, and power. Much of the writing—I'm thinking of Robert Cormier, Sharon Creech, Walter Dean Myers,

Elizabeth Berg, Madeleine L'Engle—is both exquisite and profound. More importantly, much of the sentiment expressed in contemporary adolescent fiction mirrors and celebrates . . . emerging power—that sense of independence and self—of the adolescent mind. As adults can turn to fiction for portrayals of the universalities of our condition, so our students can find their perspectives reflected and explored in a body of fiction of their own, books that can help them grow up and books that can help them love books (1998, 36).

Adolescent literature has several additional benefits. Especially compelling is the evidence that light reading can serve as a conduit to heavier reading. A poor reader will, at least initially, select materials that are congruent with his or her skill level; this light reading provides students with the motivation and the reading skills that make more difficult reading possible. A review of the research shows that many children who do extensive free reading eventually choose what experts have decided are "good books," and they expand their reading interests as they read more (Krashen 1993). This is important since reading ability is related to reading materials—whereas good readers prefer abstract, imaginative, and complex material, poor readers prefer material that is more concrete.

Exposure to a Wide Variety of Materials

Although an awareness of adolescent reading interests and the interests of particular students is important—with many reluctant readers needing high-interest, low-level reading material to motivate them to read—the concern that students *broaden* their interests must also be addressed.

Some tips for broadening interests are:

- Provide reading material in the classroom that reflects a wide range of interests and reading difficulty.

- Invite local authors to talk about books they have written; also invite parents or community members to share special interests or hobbies, and try to link these interests to books in the school library.

- Use movies to stimulate interest in different subjects, and introduce books that relate to these subjects.

- Have students give "book talks" about the books they are reading to small groups of students. A successful book talk program includes the following: teacher modeling of book talks, establishing heterogeneous groups of five to six student book talkers, and dramatic oral readings of exciting passages (Moscrip 1991). Students giving book talks in content-area classrooms might select biographies of renowned historical figures or scientists, current events articles, or works of fiction that either recreate a historical period or bring a content-area concept to life.

Educators should be concerned not only with diversifying students' reading *interests*, but also with diversifying the *types* of materials that students read. For example, in a social studies classroom, students might read newspaper articles, stories about people from different cultures or times, or travel guides in addition to the textbooks. The importance of this factor is underscored by research involving teacher experience. One study found experienced content-area teachers are less likely to depend on the textbook to structure their lessons than are relatively inexperienced teachers; for example, less-experienced teachers often rely on textual information for lectures or discussions (Menke and Davey 1994).

Sustained Silent Reading

Time available for reading is also a factor to consider. In the teenage years, opportunities for new activities abound, such as clubs, dating, sports, music, and social events; at the same time, the homework load is likely to increase. Regrettably, all of these activities take time away from pleasure reading. Perhaps the only way to encourage adolescents to read for fun is to set aside time for free reading during the school day. Moreover, making time for students' independent reading serves as a demonstration that reading is a high-priority concern to teachers and schools.

In a Sustained Silent Reading (SSR) program, the teacher, or even the entire school, sets aside a certain period of time during the day or week in which students can read books of their choice. Students can select material from the school library or from the classroom bookshelf, or even bring in reading of their own choosing. Teachers should read silently along with the students, rather than using the time to complete paperwork, because this reinforces the concept that reading is an important activity. Following the reading period, teachers may ask students to write in response journals about what they have read. Many advocates of free reading, however, caution against holding students accountable for what is read, because doing so may discourage a reluctant reader.

SSR is a critical tool for developing the automaticity, fluency, vocabulary, and background knowledge of all readers—low achieving and high achieving alike (Greenwood 2002; Hirsch 2003). Students should engage in SSR for approximately 200 minutes per week (100 minutes at school and at home), using texts they can read at a 95 percent accuracy level (Whittier and Blokker 2001).

One challenge in implementing SSR is that students are sometimes distracted or unmotivated to read. To address this concern, teachers should provide clear demonstrations of their expectations for SSR, showing students what it looks like and sounds like. For example, teachers can provide a good-natured dramatization of what distraction looks like (tapping pencils, passing notes, daydreaming). Some silent reading guidelines teachers might present to students include:

- Always have plenty of reading material. If you are about to finish a book, choose another one that you will read next.

- Try to read as much as you can—time for silent reading is limited, and you need to make the most of it.

- Avoid sitting by someone who is likely to distract you (Williams 2001).

Many struggling readers need extra support with silent reading: they may benefit from personalized teacher instruction in order to get started. This might include talking one-on-one with the student about selecting books that are at the right level (Broadus and Ivey 2002) or demonstrating ways students can check the level of difficulty of books.

Reading Aloud

Reading aloud is a common activity in elementary schools. Research supports the notion that this activity is crucial for elementary school children, indicating that children who are read to at home read more on their own and demonstrate increased comprehension, vocabulary, and interest in reading (Krashen 1993).

While many secondary school teachers view this activity as a time waster not suited to adolescents (Ecroyd 1991), reading aloud to secondary students can have substantive benefits, as this teacher describes:

> First, it helps students feel a sense of belonging to a community of readers. Our shared experiences with read-aloud texts bring us

together at least once a day to laugh, cry, and wonder as a group. Students do not have to do anything with the read-aloud text except enjoy it. For some, this is a new experience. Second, I frequently model my thinking while reading aloud to students. They hear me stop to reflect on parts of the reading that make me wonder or confuse me. Students get to hear what I do to clear up confusion and misunderstandings while I read. Often, I use the read-aloud to model the strategies students learn in minilessons (Williams 2001).

Also, oral readings of classics such as Shakespearean plays can be instrumental to generating interest in classic literature. Some suggested guidelines for teachers who want to develop a read-aloud program for teenagers include:

- Read the book first, to be sure it is something you like and want to share with others. Although students may not like everything you like, they won't be interested in a book if you aren't.

- Select passages that are powerful (suspenseful, gory, hilarious, or romantic).

- Before beginning the read-aloud session, relate the work to something the teenagers know about.

- Stop reading before students stop listening—the oral reader should constantly monitor the interest of listeners and their body language. At the first sign of boredom, either move on to another activity, increase the drama in your voice, or skip some passages to get to the good parts quickly.

- Give listeners an opportunity to respond to what has been read, and emphasize the importance of a nonthreatening atmosphere while they are responding (Matthews 1987).

The Read-Aloud Books Too Good to Miss program is a project of the Association for Indiana Media Educators. Five read-aloud lists, including one each for middle and high school, are developed each year. Lists for several years are available at http://www.ilfonline.org/Units/Associations/aime/Programs/ReadAlouds/Readaloud.htm.

Reading aloud is especially beneficial for at-risk students. It can provide these students, some of whom have never finished a book, with the sense of enjoyment that comes from reading and completing a book. Ivey suggests that read-alouds can also provide an opportunity for teachers to model what they do as they read silently:

> You ask yourself questions, hypothesize and predict, make connections to what you already know and to what you have read, relate the information to personal experiences, and keep a check on whether or not you truly understand as you read. Engaging students in these processes with you as you read to them not only helps them think about the text but also tips them off to how they can read more thoughtfully on their own (2003, 813).

Opportunities can also be provided for *students* to read aloud in the content-area classroom. One structured approach is Rapid Retrieval of Information, or RRI (Green 1998). Students begin by reading the text silently in class. Then the teacher poses questions that require recall as well as higher-level thinking skills such as drawing inferences and analyzing. Students skim the reading to search for answers, and the teacher calls on volunteers as well as non-volunteers to read aloud the words or paragraphs that contain the answer to the question. Green writes: "The combination of using higher level thinking skills, scanning information, and reading aloud highly motivates most of my students" (1998, 307). Additionally, RRI provides the teacher with valuable diagnostic information regarding students' decoding skills, fluency, comprehension, and ability to skim information.

Talking About Texts

When we think about the activity of reading, the image that comes to mind for most of us is that of a solitary reader curled up in a chair, engrossed in a book, oblivious to the rest of the world. Yet, reading is rarely a purely solitary phenomenon. Even when we read a book by ourselves, it is often in a social context, such as in a classroom, a library, or at home in the presence of family members, where a potential exists for sharing the reading experience. Books can serve as a catalyst for social interactions between the reader and others. For example, one might select books based on a friend's advice or discuss a book with others who have read it. Adolescents experience the social aspect of reading through activities such as joining book clubs, discussing teen romance novels during lunch periods, and picking up books that a sibling has checked out of the library.

A wide assortment of activities that highlight the social nature of reading can be introduced in the classroom, such as book talks (see page 29), group projects as part of a thematic unit (see page 43), and small-group discussions.

Small-Group Discussion

Small student groups assembled to discuss works of literature (or other reading materials) can be highly effective in enhancing both reading comprehension and interpretation, as has been shown in studies involving both elementary and secondary students (Sweigart 1991; Nystrand, Gamoran, and Heck 1993; Leal 1992). Students in one study reported that discussion assisted them to become engaged with ideas, construct meaning, and take responsibility for their own learning (Alvermann et al. 1996). Furthermore, this type of learning strategy has been found to be superior to lecture or whole-class discussion in facilitating the understanding of complex ideas (Sweigart 1991).

To be effective, small-group work should be carefully designed. One element that seems to affect the instructional effectiveness of small groups is the amount of autonomy students receive. Nystrand, Gamoran, and Heck (1993) compared the effects of different types of small-group work on achievement in the study of literature, and they found that autonomous groups (in which the students in the group define and resolve the problem) are more effective than problem-solving groups (in which students are required to come to a consensus about a problem defined by the teacher), which are in turn more effective than "collaborative seatwork" (an activity highly structured by the teacher, such as completing worksheets in a group). The authors recommend that teachers design small-group assignments that specify the parameters of the activities, yet allow the students themselves to determine the precise nature of the activities.

In Alvermann et al.'s 1996 study of middle and high school students' perceptions of text-based discussions, many of the students expressed the opinion that a certain degree of student autonomy was critical. One of the themes that emerged was that the best discussions center around a mutual exploration of ideas, with these often productive and relevant to the content at hand even if they strayed from the teacher's original intentions.

However, Nystrand, Gamoran, and Heck advise teachers to keep in mind that, while small-group discussions are particularly appropriate for certain educational goals, they are less appropriate for other goals. For example, a lecture-style class format may more effectively introduce a great deal of new information. Worksheets may be appropriate at times when the teacher wants students to practice a newly developed skill. But, as the authors write, "If teachers want students to compare ideas, develop a train of thought, air differences, or arrive at a consensus on some controversial issue, then the forum of small groups may be just the right setting for most students to carry on intensive conversation" (1993, 22).

Benefits of small discussion groups include:

- These groups take advantage of the social nature of secondary students.

- In carefully designed discussion groups, a high proportion of students speak. One researcher found that 90 percent or more of students spoke during a student-led discussion format (Knoeller 1994).

- Discussion groups support the development of skills such as cooperation, inquiry, problem solving, and communication.

- Students who participate in these groups typically do more than just receive information; they are also placed in the role of expert or resource. The implicit message is that developing their own thoughts—not just remembering someone else's—is important.

- When reading independently, struggling readers often make irrelevant associations that interfere with comprehension. Such learners need to hear other viewpoints and compare them with their own thinking to improve their understanding (Collins 1996).

Designing Small-Group Work

When first establishing the small-group discussion format, teachers are often concerned about whether or not students will talk, if one student will dominate the discussion, or if students will have difficulty keeping the conversation focused on the text. Here are some tips for designing and supporting discussion groups:

- Group size ideally should be between four and eight—large enough to bring diversity of opinion, but small enough to ensure all students can participate fully (Wiencek and O'Flahavan 1994).

- Accept that not all discussion will be focused on higher-level thinking. Sometimes enthusiastic conversations that are only superficially related to the text serve the purpose of providing an "easy entry into the discussion" and putting teenagers in an "active, evaluative role" (Roller and Beed 1994).

- How often should groups be changed? Seek students' advice on when they see the need to rearrange groups, but keep in mind students may need time to establish their group dynamic and interactive norms (Wiencek and O'Flahavan 1994).

Gauthier (1989) provides some additional guidelines that could be used for reading groups in the content areas. Before forming the groups, first limit the amount of text to be read at one time—it ideally should be only a short selection. Activate prior knowledge and introduce key vocabulary. Then, ask students to read the selection and write responses to these three items: 1) What have you learned from reading this selection? 2) How does the information in this selection connect to the other things you know about this subject? and 3) List the words in the selection that you do not fully understand. After the students discuss these questions in small groups and write their responses, the teacher should join in the discussion, either by moving from one group to another, or by assembling the students in a whole-class discussion.

Scott (1994) suggests that the assignment of roles to students in literature discussion groups can provide a helpful framework for encouraging students to focus on different facets of the reading process. In a framework developed by Scott, each student assumes a role such as those described below:

- Discussion Director—Designs and discusses questions about the text.

- Passage Master—Notes and shares important passages.

- Connector—Makes connections between the book and real life.

- Illustrator—Illustrates and shares an important part of the story.

- Scene Setter—Tracks and describes the settings in the story.

- Character Captain—Responds to the actions of the characters.

- Word Wizard—Defines and discusses interesting or confusing words.

- Summarizer—Briefly summarizes the key points.

These role structures could also be suitable for non-fiction materials. For example, a group discussing a science article or textbook chapter could potentially use the roles above, with the likely exceptions of Scene Setter and Character Captain.

One way to promote autonomy in small discussion groups is to encourage students to conduct independent research after discussing topics that are of great interest to them. For example, when one teacher designed literature circles around social issues such as child abuse and war, some students still had so many questions after the discussion that they were motivated to extend their own learning through interviews and research.

Using Discussion Groups with At-Risk and Remedial Readers

Discussion groups are particularly appropriate for at-risk and remedial readers. Too often, these students are viewed from the perspective of their weaknesses, and it is assumed that the personal experiences they bring to the classroom have little merit (Gentile and McMillan 1994). Discussion groups call upon the firsthand knowledge of these students to interpret a text, underscoring the value of their personal experiences.

When designing small-group work for at-risk students, some modifications may be necessary. Shorter amounts of text may be more appropriate than a whole book for a reading assignment. If the students have had little experience with small-group instruction, teachers should specifically address the ground rules for conducting a discussion when introducing the activity. In addition, the teacher might work with the entire class at first, until students acclimate themselves to the activity; students might then be divided into smaller groups for discussion of the reading (Gentile and McMillan 1994).

To help struggling readers develop their discussion skills, teachers often must do more than simply pose questions for students to answer. An effective technique is to initially model both questions and answers, which provides these readers with critical exposure to comprehension processes and clarifies the discussion task. After ample modeling for *all* students, teachers can gradually diminish the support and transfer responsibility to students (Curran 1997).

Note Cue is a method that provides students with support in their initial attempts to participate in discussion groups (Manzo and Manzo 1990). It is suitable for any students who seem to be struggling, including students who speak English as a second language. Note Cue tells students *what* they might say in class discussion, leaving them only to think about *when* they should say it. The advantage of this strategy is that it "builds behaviors by first producing an appropriate behavior where previously there were none, or only inappropriate ones" (1990, 609).

To implement Note Cue, the teacher gives students notecards that contain teacher-developed questions, answers, and comments that might be made during discussion of a particular text. The teacher then invites pupils to first read questions, then the answers that might fit the questions, and then the appropriate comments. The students must decide at what point in the discussion their contributions are appropriate. The reading of teacher-prepared notecards may seem like mindless parroting, but in fact it has the potential to make students feel more competent, in that they develop situationally appropriate behaviors for discussion participation. The strategy includes specific ways to gradually foster the learner's independence—for example, the teacher could write suggestions on the notecards that students ask certain kinds of questions, such as questions that raise doubt.

Collaborative Strategic Reading

Collaborative Strategic Reading (CSR) is a cooperative learning-based program that has been shown to improve reading comprehension. In their study of average, low-achieving, and reading-disabled middle schoolers, Vaughn, Klinger, and Bryant (2001) found CSR helped students comprehend text, learn content, and pass high-stakes tests. The four basic strategies of CSR are:

- activate background knowledge and make predictions before reading;

- monitor reading and enhance vocabulary development during reading;

- identify main ideas during reading; and

- summarize key ideas after reading.

The teacher first teaches each step in the strategy to the class as a whole. Next, a small group of students models it for the class. Then students are divided into small heterogeneous groups or pairs to apply the strategies with text. Klinger and Vaughn suggest that, after reading and small-group work, students:

> take turns sharing what they learned with the class. Many students can share their best idea in a short period of time, providing the

teacher with valuable information about each student's level of understanding (1998, 35).

Cultivating the Reading-Writing Connection

Most people would agree there is a strong connection between reading and writing, and what we read influences our choices of writing topics, as well as the genres of our written work and our writing style. In addition, those who read well often also write well, and both skilled reading and writing have been linked to reflective behaviors and metacognitive awareness.

In secondary classrooms, writing is most often used for evaluative purposes (Sensenbaugh 1990). Another potential, yet often overlooked, function of writing is to help students learn material. The National Commission on Writing in America's Schools and Colleges highlights the importance of this other role writing can play: "Writing is not simply a way for students to demonstrate what they know. It is a way to help them understand what they know. At its best, writing is learning" (2003, 13).

Turner elaborates:

> To ensure understanding of what they are reading, students should be asked to respond to this more complex reading material—to produce their own analysis of the content, to evaluate its argument or position, and to formulate their own position statements on the topic. Students will need to know how to outline and how to organize their ideas in a coherent and persuasive manner. By engaging in different types of writing, they will better understand different types of reading mate-rial. For example, an assignment that requires a student to take a point of view and to write a persuasive argument better prepares him to be a critical reader (2003, 2).

The term *writing* actually refers to a variety of activities. In-school writing might mean any of the following: writing a summary of a textbook chapter; expressing oneself in a dialogue journal; writing an essay; revising a draft of a paper; or editing a peer's work. Moreover, writing can be integrated with reading in several different ways. Writing might be a pre-reading activity (such as jotting down associations with the Ice Age before reading about it), or a post-reading activity (such as analyzing the structure of a Robert Frost poem).

Writing as a Pre-Reading Activity

Pre-reading activities increase student engagement with reading material by activating what students already know about a topic. For example, in individual or group brainstorming sessions, students might make associations with the concepts they will read about. Or students could write down their personal thoughts or experiences that relate to the topic. Autobiographical writing before reading increases understanding of a text, engagement in discussion, and understanding of characters; also, students who write before reading stories tend to like the stories better (White 1992). This technique could be used as easily in any content-area classroom. For example, when beginning the study of geometry, the teacher could ask students to write down some things they already know about shapes.

Dialogue Journals

A dialogue journal is an informal, written conversation between a student and another person (usually a teacher, but it could also be a peer or parent), in which participants chat, either about issues of importance to them or about the material they are reading. Benefits of using dialogue journals include:

- Students have an opportunity to write for a genuine audience.

- Teachers have one-on-one time with students that otherwise might not be feasible.

- Dialogue in these journals has the potential to go beyond the parameters of usual classroom discourse because the conversation is more private, and those who are shy or unsure about the value of their own ideas express themselves more readily.

Dialogue journals are an effective way to get students involved with their texts, because the goal of such journals is not to write polished essays, but to express honest responses to texts and to become more aware of the reading process without having to worry about elements such as grammar and punctuation. The benefits of dialogue journals are underscored by a case study of two veteran English teachers who introduced them in their classrooms (Gross 1992). Both teachers found the students enjoyed this activity, became more eager to read, were more engaged in reading, and liked sharing ideas with peers.

Guidelines for students who write in reading dialogue journals should include:

- Express your personal responses to reading—your opinions, feelings, likes, and dislikes.

- Relate the book to your own experiences; write about similar things that have happened to you.

- Don't worry about spelling and grammar. Expressing your thoughts is more important.

- Feel free to talk about things you don't understand, or ask questions about what is happening or why something is happening.

- Make predictions about what will happen in the rest of the book. As you continue reading, keep track of which predictions came true, but don't worry about being wrong.

- Praise or criticize the book, giving specific reasons why you feel this way, such as the writing style or subject matter (Fuhler 1994; Wells 1993).

Because teachers are flexible about grammar and other language rules when reading the dialogue journals, those students who are not native English speakers may feel more free to write than they might when given other writing assignments. Students speaking very little English could even draw pictures to express their ideas, to which teachers might respond initially with pictures and a few words. Dialogue journals can also provide opportunities for exchanging cultural knowledge between people of different backgrounds.

Journals may be used in conjunction with an independent reading program, as a forum for discussing books students have chosen. Conversations can be recorded in a notebook (preferably a spiral bound one, in order to resist wear and tear). At the back of the notebook, students can keep a log of what they have read and when they completed a reading. This serves as an easy reference for teachers, readers, and parents.

Students should write regularly in dialogue journals—ideally at least once a week. Because dialogue journals require regular reading and responding from teachers, time management is an important concern. Keep in mind, however, that dialogue journals are not simply an added demand on teaching load. In fact, they can *replace* some kinds of written work, as one middle school teacher describes:

> I remember suffering through piles of junior high book reports, the dullest writing I've ever read. By contrast, the [kids'] letters are a constant source of surprise, pleasure, and stimulation. And what they replaced—book reports, worksheets, quizzes, and tests—ate up more time than keeping up with my correspondents ever will (Atwell 1998, 298).

Students should have the opportunity to write to diverse audiences, such as peers and parents. It has been found that students write different kinds of journal entries to peers than to teachers; for example, students are more likely to recommend books to one another than to teachers (Wells 1993), and they write more often about their emotional reactions to a book when writing to a peer (Atwell 1998). In addition, involving parents in the dialogue journal process is a powerful way to link home and school (Fuhler 1994).

The Reading-Writing Connection in the Content Areas

There are several ways to foster the reading-writing connection in the content areas. The time investment for these activities may seem great, but it can pay off by providing teachers with valuable information on how much their students comprehend, as well as by increasing student engagement with the text. Some suggestions (International Reading Association 1990) are:

- *Journal writing.* Set aside time at the end of class, perhaps five minutes, for students to engage in this activity. Teachers might ask pupils to write in their journals about their own classroom learning experiences, to explain concepts in their own words, or to pose questions.

- *Free writing.* This pre-reading strategy invites students to describe what they know about a topic before studying it. Following this brainstorming session, students could share their ideas with the rest of the class.

- *Creation of possible sentences.* This technique is a tool for making meaning from technical vocabulary and content-area concepts. Teachers first display key vocabulary that is defined in a passage to be read; students use key vocabulary to predict sentences that may appear in the lesson and then read the lesson to verify the sentences they have written, evaluating them for accuracy and correcting errors.

Other Approaches

Interactive approaches to reading instruction might also include structured classroom debates and thematic units. These types of activities often call upon students to use critical thinking skills in interpreting their reading materials. Using computers to promote reading instruction is another approach that, when carefully designed, can be highly effective.

Classroom Debate

Teachers often avoid provoking academic conflicts among students, either because such conflicts are perceived as divisive, or because an instructional model is not readily available. However, structured classroom controversies have been shown to result in greater student mastery of the subject, as well as an increase in the quality and number of ideas, creative insight, and student enjoyment (Johnson and Johnson 1988). Moreover, in-class debate is particularly well suited to adolescent learners, because:

> Teenagers have a natural propensity toward questioning, challenging, and arguing as they seek to establish who they are, what they believe in, what they want to accomplish, and what they expect from life. This process of moving from strong parental influence to the more powerful peer influence is a very active one. Teaching methods that acknowledge and capitalize on this stage of human development can be very effective.... One such method that gets students actively involved in discussing literature is debate (Schauer and Beyersdorfer 1992, 57).

Opportunities to debate could be provided in the content-area classroom in a number of ways. For instance, students could debate environmental issues in science class, take the sides of political candidates in social studies class, or even debate the uses and misuses of statistical polls in math or social studies classes, with some written material suggested by the teacher as source documents. The four steps listed below provide one possible structure for designing student debates:

1) Introduce the class to the idea of a planned controversy and the need to resolve it; remind them of the importance of respecting opinions different from their own.

2) Establish a background for the controversy. Ask students to read textbooks and primary source materials.

3) Determine which side each student will be on. Students may take the side they actually support, or they may be randomly assigned. Remind students that a good debater can argue for either side of an issue. Ask students to find evidence for their side in the material they have read.

4) Involve students in a simulation where they are forced to take a position on the controversy. The format for the debate might include opening statements, presentation of arguments, rebuttals, and closing statements. If a winner is to be chosen, ask observing students to keep track of which team presented more arguments that were not successfully rebutted by the other team (Schauer and Beyersdorfer 1992).

This approach not only requires reading by the students, but also demands that they process what they read in a way that utilizes higher order skills.

Thematic Units

In a thematic unit, a topic or theme provides the focus for study. Thematic units can be implemented in all the content areas with the themes that most interest adolescents, including those that grapple with difficult issues, such as the effects of technology on society (Weaver 1994). The advantage of a thematic approach is not only that it integrates various areas of a discipline by relating them to a theme, but also that it lends itself to using a wide range of reading materials written at different difficulty levels. A wide variety of activities, varying from individual written work and small-group creative projects to in-class dramatizations, can be incorporated in this approach.

For example, a thematic unit on the American Revolution could include whole-class or small-group activities such as creating a timeline of pictures depicting major events of the American Revolution, acting out the courtroom scene from the novel *Johnny Tremain*, writing letters to the editor for or against the Boston Tea Party, or producing a classroom edition of the *Boston Observer* newspaper as it might have appeared during that period (Weaver 1994).

Thematic units can vary in the extent of student involvement. When students have a major role in planning the thematic unit—identifying main ideas and finding resources—they feel a sense of ownership of the project and are more likely to invest themselves in the process of learning (Weaver 1994). Greater student participation in the planning does not, however, mean teacher responsibility for planning is lessened. In fact, shifting more responsibility to students often requires that a teacher be more organized, in order to ensure the learning potential provided by the activity contributes to the unit's goals.

Another way of structuring reading activities within a thematic unit is to assign students to read one book together as a class and then allow each student to select another related book. To guide students in choosing relevant books, the teacher can design a list of books, keeping student interest in mind. After the teacher introduces the books by providing brief information on each one, each student chooses a book and reads it in class. This approach is called Guided Independent Reading; Podl (1995) reports that the student choice component fosters a sense of ownership and pleasure in reading.

Reader's Theater

Readers can enhance their understanding of story characters and plot through the technique of Reader's Theater. One way of approaching Reader's Theater is for students to assume the roles of characters and pantomime the characters' personalities and emotions, perhaps reenacting important conversations between different characters. Students could also take roles and read the text aloud as a script, using their vocal expression and discourse style to recreate the characters. After the Reader's Theater performance, classmates could discuss whether the reenactment reflected their own understanding of the characters and plot, referring to the text itself to support their interpretation. This approach gives students an important opportunity to practice reading toward a goal (Curran 1997; Ivey 1999).

Concept-Oriented Reading Instruction

The CORI approach emphasizes a wide variety of reading strategies during all stages of the activity, such as notetaking, skimming, summarizing, activating prior knowledge, and identifying main ideas. Teachers are actively involved in helping students use these strategies as tools to help them reach their goals.

The intent of Concept-Oriented Reading Instruction (CORI) is to develop motivation and set the stage for reading. For example, students might observe the plant and animal life in a park, handle fossils, visit a historical landmark, or build a replica of a Native American totem pole in their classroom. If this real-world observation sparks curiosity, students will read, write, and discuss their observations and reflections with enthusiasm. The curiosity will then develop into a set of personalized questions, which the students can seek to answer through reading relevant books in the classroom library. After retrieving information, students integrate the resources into coherent answers to their questions and communicate the answers to the rest of the class (Guthrie et al. 1999).

Technology and Reading Instruction

With the advent of the information age, computerized instruction has begun to play a critical role in our schools, and several studies have shown that computers can be useful and motivating tools for reading instruction.

The effectiveness of computer-assisted reading instruction depends largely on the type of computer programs used. The most effective programs are those that provide students with whole texts, foster active involvement, or include opportunities for learners to make decisions that influence the computer task—rather than "locking" teachers and students into drill-and-practice exercises that emphasize isolated language fragments (Simic 1993).

Well-designed computer-assisted reading instruction can offer several important benefits (Kamil 2003; Divine and Whanger 1990; DeGroff 1990; Wepner, 1990):

- It gives students a sense of control.

- Students enjoy graphics and animation.

- Students often report that working with the computer is fun, and that they are motivated to read.

- Students can progress at their own rate, separate from the pace of the rest of the class.

- Students experience immediate reinforcement for their work.

- Computers provide opportunities for social interaction, either through pairing students up at computers or through use of telecommunication.

- When students can communicate with others via tools such as electronic mail, they have a real purpose for writing and reading, and a real audience and the opportunity to practice the "conventions of 'written conversations'" (Kamil 2003, 24).

- Activities can easily be structured to provide collaborative opportunities.

- Computer-assisted reading instruction can reduce fear of failure and so be especially helpful for at-risk adolescents.

An approach to using computers to increase reading skills was reported through use of a computerized reading management and enrichment program. Students chose and read books from a list of 900 works of classic literature, then took an individualized test on a computer. The computer tracked their reading progress and generated reading reports for teachers, parents, and students. The program was carefully designed: it accommodated a wide range of reading levels, it was noncompetitive in nature, tests were motivational as well as instructional, and students were able to read and be tested at their own pace. The researchers compared the scores of students at a school that implemented this program with the scores of students at a similar school in the district that did *not* implement the program. Not only did they find that the program significantly increased reading achievement, they also found that it increased the number of books read per week, and that a majority of students liked the approach (Peak and Dewalt 1994).

Computer-assisted reading instruction can also be implemented with simple word processing software. For example, one way to help students extract meaning from texts is to teach them how to color code word-processed texts for meaning. Students might select different colors for different types of sentences and phrases, such as topic sentences, opinions versus facts, or descriptions versus narratives. If color coding is done on the computer rather than with highlighter pens, students will have the opportunity to reconsider and redo their coding, and then possibly print out their final result on a color printer (Viau 1998).

With the proliferation of Web sites, many educational materials that can be used to supplement texts can be found on the Internet. To help ensure students comprehend what they are reading, a set of guided questions about the text can be prepared and provided to them.

Computers can also provide a highly motivating approach to connecting reading and writing in the curriculum. For example, one teacher made the text of a passage available as a computerized document, and then gave students guidance in specific ways to manipulate the text on the computer screen, such as adding their own thoughts and questions, or reorganizing the concepts within the material (Bernhardt 1994). This approach encourages interaction with the material, and gives readers a sense of ownership. An analysis of research studies focused on the effects of computer technology and achievement identifies another indirect benefit that may be important for struggling readers—the development of more positive attitudes toward themselves and learning (Sivin-Kachala, Bialo, and Rosso 1998).

An important point—with all of the approaches just discussed, teacher planning and guidance is the key to whether the approach provides worthwhile opportunities for student learning. For example, Kamil suggests adolescents may need help learning how to "synthesize visual and text information" (2003, 22), a format that students will encounter when accessing Web-based resources.

Developing Good Reading Comprehension Strategies

Good reading comprehension is the ultimate goal of reading instruction. It is a complex process that requires the integration of many different skills and strategies. For example, before starting to read, strategic readers automatically—although almost subconsciously—consider their prior knowledge about a subject and identify the purpose for their reading.

During reading, strategic readers: monitor their comprehension (perhaps by mentally paraphrasing the material, checking the accuracy of predictions they have made, or asking themselves questions to see whether they understand); recognize obstacles to comprehension (such as unusual writing style, too many unknown words, and lack of background information); and try to remedy problems in comprehension when they occur (perhaps by rereading the passage or changing reading speed). Interestingly, although strategic readers are highly aware of their thinking and reading processes, their approach to reading is often implicit, and they may not be aware that what they are doing would be termed a strategy.

Poor readers—or, more generally, poor learners—demonstrate much lower levels of competence with comprehension strategies. Even when attending to the mechanics of the task at hand, they may have little idea of the reasons for doing it, how to approach its solution, or how their efforts relate to outcomes. This lack of understanding of the learning process may present an even greater barrier to learning than deficits in some of the basic skills needed for a particular content area. On a more positive note, students can be taught good reading strategies if they are explicitly explained, modeled, and regularly incorporated into classrooms (Helfeldt and Henk 1990; Smith 1992). Once learned and applied, they are tools that can be used in situations both inside and outside classrooms. As such they should also be considered valuable products of the learning process.

Metacognitive Behaviors of Good and Poor Readers		
	Good Readers	**Poor Readers**
Before reading	• Activate prior knowledge • Understand task and set purpose • Choose appropriate strategies	• Start reading without preparation • Read without knowing why • Read without considering how to approach material
During reading	• Focus attention • Anticipate and predict • Use fix-up strategies when lack of understanding occurs • Use contextual analysis to understand new terms • Use text structure to assist comprehension • Organize and integrate new information • Self-monitor comprehension by knowing comprehension is occurring and knowing what is being understood	• Are easily distracted • Read to get done • Do not know what to do when lack of understanding occurs • Do not recognize important vocabulary • Do not see any organization • Add on, rather than integrate, new information • Do not realize they do not understand
After reading	• Reflect on what was read • Feel success is a result of effort • Summarize major ideas • Seek outside information from outside sources	• Stop reading and thinking • Feel success is a result of luck

Source: Fuentes 1998, 83.

Some of the basic skills that underlie comprehension strategies are:

• *Predicting.* Predictions encourage students to read with a purpose and to confirm or correct their predictions as they construct meaning. One strategy that uses prediction is the Directed Reading-Thinking Activity (see page 56).

• *Self-questioning.* Self-questioning allows learners to actively check how much they understand while reading. Students can pose questions such as *What is the main idea?* and *Are there examples to help clarify the main idea?* Students who generate their own questions have been shown to have greater improvement in comprehension than students who simply answer questions posed by teachers (Singer and Donlan 1982). A number of specific self-questioning strategies have been developed, such as SQ3R (see page 54).

- *Paraphrasing.* By putting the concepts of a passage or section in their own words, or by summarizing the main points, students can get a sense of how much they understand.

- *Visual representation.* Creating visual models of ideas within a text provides a means of organizing information into understandable wholes and promotes the visualization of relationships (see pages 58-59).

- *Changing reading speed.* When students encounter obstacles such as an unusual writing style or too many unknown words, they should modify their reading speed. Good readers are able to determine the appropriate pace for their purpose. For example, they can determine when it is best to quickly scan the material (frequently useful when reading the newspaper, for example), and when material is best approached with slow and deliberate reading (such as a complicated math problem).

Pre-Reading Activities

Three important objectives of pre-reading activities are to:

1) get students to think about what they already know about a topic;

2) direct their attention to a purpose for which they will be reading; and

3) spark their interest and curiosity in the topic (Ciborowski 1992).

Types of pre-reading activities that teachers might implement include:

- *Oral previews.* Components include: short questions and statements designed to catch the students' interest and provide a link between a familiar topic and the story's topic; story synopsis; introduction of characters; and definition of unfamiliar words. Oral previewing has been shown to improve both comprehension and recall.

- *Introducing core vocabulary.* Students will encounter new words and terms in their reading (particularly if they are reading in a content area). An introduction to the most important vocabulary terms makes the reading more approachable and gives students an idea of what the reading will be about.

- *Autobiographical writing before reading.* Students can write down their own personal experiences that relate to the topic. Autobiographical writing before reading enhances understanding of the text, as well as engagement in discussion and understanding of characters (White 1992).

- *Writing down predictions.* Students predict what they think they will learn; after reading the text, they write what they actually did learn.

- *Anticipation guides.* Students answer five or more teacher-prepared true-false statements about major concepts within the topic they are about to study. These guides are more likely to motivate reluctant readers if they include controversial statements or statements that challenge students to examine their beliefs. Student responses also will help the teacher determine which misperceptions need to be corrected in the course of study—this is an important step in enhancing students' comprehension (Barton 1997).

- *Drawing analogies.* When students lack important background knowledge, teachers can use analogy as an interpretive bridge between unfamiliar material and what students do know. Using analogies as a pre-reading strategy improves students' recall and prediction skills.

- *Brainstorming about initial associations with key concepts.* This activity can help to improve story comprehension since it assists students in making links between already-known and new material.

When instruction helps readers activate prior knowledge, attention becomes better focused on a reason for reading. Ciborowski writes "reading becomes more gratifying because its purpose is now more apparent" (1992, 34). In fact, setting a purpose for reading is critical to good reading skills. Langer (1993) studied the approaches to literary understanding among secondary readers, and concluded that what sets better readers apart from poorer readers is a tendency to think about the primary purpose for reading. Poorer readers lacked "a vision of the kind of knowledge they are after in the first place" (36). One way to focus on the purpose for reading is to use the KWL strategy, in which students make lists of what they **K**now, what they **W**ant to know, and then what they **L**earned.

Useful Strategies during Reading

Numerous strategies have been developed to help readers monitor their comprehension, and new strategies are continually being developed. Several examples of comprehension strategies are described below. It is important to introduce only one or two reading strategies at a time, when earlier ones have been internalized. Mastery of any of these strategies may take several days of practice.

"Click or Clunk" Strategy

This is a particularly useful strategy when working with nonfiction. At the end of a section of reading, students should ask themselves if the meaning of a text "clicks" for them or if it goes "clunk." If it clunks, they should ask what they can do to make sense of it. Weaver writes: "This is a delightfully simple yet effective way of getting readers to stop their reading and rethink rather than continuing to read without comprehension. It is most likely to be adopted by students if the teacher repeatedly demonstrates how he or she uses it, and teachers and students use it collectively" (1994, 157).

Reciprocal Teaching

The reciprocal teaching strategy engages teachers and students in a process of asking each other questions about the text. Reciprocal teaching might occur as students and teachers read a passage of material, paragraph by paragraph. During the reading, they periodically take time out to ask each other questions and monitor their comprehension (Palincsar and Herrenkohl 2003).

There are two phases to this strategy. The first step is instruction in the use of four comprehension-monitoring strategies: summarization, question generation, clarification, and prediction. At first, the teacher assumes most of the responsibility for instruction. In the second phase, however, the students begin to take on more responsibility—they ask questions, request clarification of material they don't understand, make predictions about what will happen next, and summarize what they have read (Rosenshine and Meister 1994).

Research demonstrates the efficacy of reciprocal teaching in fostering reading comprehension in the context of a remedial reading classroom (Alfassi 1998) as well as in a general education science classroom (Spiak 1999). The reciprocal teaching strategy offers several advantages to learners. Because students can witness which questions the teacher thinks are worth asking, they have a model available for the questions that they themselves will formulate.

Through using this strategy, students discover information sources for questions and develop the habit of self-questioning. In addition, students are put into the unique position of being able to assume a teaching role. This contrasts sharply with the more traditional student role of answering questions posed in the text or by the teacher.

Slater and Horstman (2002) offer the following cautions about using reciprocal teaching:

- Often students ask a disproportionate number of literal questions, with too few clarification questions—which suggests students are not adequately monitoring their comprehension. Therefore, teachers need to continually monitor student progress and move them from literal questions to thought-provoking ones, for example questions that ask students to find the main idea, or make conclusions, predictions, or comparisons.

- As the teacher hands more responsibility for instruction to the students, he or she should monitor student progress carefully and be willing to step in and provide more modeling or explanation when needed.

Teachers might enhance students' reading comprehension by pairing reciprocal teaching with an intervention called Paragraph Patterns (Spiak 1999). Science teachers in one school found that when reciprocal teaching was first introduced, most students speed-read through the material and did not remember the concepts well. To hold students more accountable for what they read, the teachers implemented Paragraph Patterns, an approach that involves identifying and writing down the main idea of a paragraph. Content comprehension scores more than doubled after the intervention, and students were better able to identify the main idea of passages.

SQ3R

This is a well-known strategy that involves skills such as summarizing, self-questioning, and text lookback. There are five steps:

- *Survey*: Skim a chapter for general understanding before reading it.

- *Question*: Formulate questions using the chapter's boldface headings.

- *Read*: Read a section to locate answers to the questions that have been formulated.

Strategy Reference Cards

Casteel, Isom, and Jordan suggest that providing students with strategy reference cards—or having them develop their own—can remind students how to use a strategy until it becomes a natural part of their learning repertoire. They provide this example.

Using Fix-Up Strategies: What to do when I don't understand.

Choose one of these.

- Ignore and read on.

- Guess by context.

- Reread to clear up confusion.

- Look back to previous information. See if it helps me understand the difficult part (2000, 71).

- *Recite*: Paraphrase main ideas and supporting details, and check them against the passage.

- *Review*: Recall main points before reading subheadings; recall as much supporting information as possible (Call 1991).

SCAN & RUN

This instructional framework consists of cues for strategies that help students plan and monitor their comprehension before, during, and after reading expository text. Instruction in the use of SCAN & RUN has resulted in higher scores on homework, quizzes, and tests for low, average, and high achievers; moreover, both teachers and students expressed high satisfaction with this strategy (Salembier 1999).

Before reading, students use four SCAN cues while previewing chapter text:

S = Survey headings and turn them into questions (students will answer the questions during the reading).

C = Capture the captions and visuals (reading the captions and looking at the visual clues to try to understand what each means).

A = Attack boldface words (reading boldface words, which are usually key vocabulary words, and figuring out what they mean).

N = Note and read the chapter questions (reading the questions at the end of the chapter so that they can be kept in mind while reading the chapter).

While reading the chapter, students use the three RUN cues:

R = Read and adjust speed (adjust reading speed depending on the difficulty of the section).

U = Use word identification skills such as sounding it out, looking for other word clues in the sentence, or breaking words into parts for unknown words.

N = Notice and check parts you don't understand and reread or read on (place a check mark next to the part you don't understand, and decide to reread that section or skip it and go back to it after you're finished reading).

After reading, students extend their understanding of the text by answering questions about and discussing the text.

Instruction in the use of SCAN & RUN involves several steps that facilitate independent use of the strategy by students. Instruction begins with a whole-class introduction to the strategy, followed by teacher modeling of a think-aloud process to illustrate how to use each SCAN & RUN cue while reading a chapter from the course text. Next are opportunities for students to memorize the seven cues through round-robin rehearsal games, and then complete a self-monitoring chart of their use of SCAN & RUN cues.

Directed Reading-Thinking Activity

The task of a Directed Reading-Thinking Activity (DR-TA) is to generate hypotheses about the material to be read, then refine these hypotheses while reading. A DR-TA is a powerful tool for fostering independence in readers, because it encourages them to use their reasoning abilities and tap their own knowledge. There are four steps to this activity:

1) *Predict.* In this stage, students reflect on what they think will be covered in the text. These predictions are recorded on the board, on an overhead projector, or on charts the students create.

2) *Read.* Students then read a few paragraphs or pages of the text.

3) *Confirm.* Students compare the predictions they made with what was actually presented in the text. (Steps one through three are repeated until the text is completed.)

4) *Resolution.* Students summarize and evaluate the text (McIntosh and Bear 1993).

IEPC Strategy

IEPC (Imagine, Elaborate, Predict, and Confirm) (Wood 2002) is a strategy similar to DR-TA. The teacher begins by modeling and explaining the strategy, describing how it can help their learning. Students are asked to:

- *Imagine.* Before reading, students explore their mental images about a topic. Everyone (including the teacher) closes their eyes and tries to imagine everything they can about the topic, including any sensory associations (smell, feeling, sight, sound, taste, surroundings). Use questions to prompt these associations.

- *Elaborate.* Model for students how to elaborate on these images and associations by thinking aloud.

- *Predict.* Based on the images and associations, develop some predictions about the text. If necessary, have students look at some of the pictures or headings in the text.

- *Confirm.* After reading the selection (while looking carefully for information to support or refute predictions), modify the predictions based on the newly learned information.

During each of these four steps, the teacher should write down students' ideas in a four-column chart, with the labels I, E, P, and C for the steps in the process.

Visual Representations

The strategy of developing visual representations of thinking processes (such as causal chains, webs, and if/then flow charts) has become popular in recent years. These kinds of visual depictions are intended to keep students focused on content and to clarify the learning task. In addition, they momentarily freeze the learning process so that students can observe the process itself. They can be highly effective learning tools; one district reports that after visual representations were introduced, student scores on a state reading test increased dramatically (Peresich, Meadows, and Sinatra 1990).

When using this strategy, teachers need to carefully consider what kind of representation to employ for a specific task. Different visual representations support different ways of thinking about a topic, thereby supporting different learning styles as well as deeper learning about the topic. For example, time lines help students arrange events chronologically; web diagrams help them tie related ideas to one concept; pro/con charts help students weigh evidence; and if/then flow charts let them work out steps in deciding between two or more choices. If the teacher first perceives and conceptualizes the material to be presented or read, he or she can determine the most appropriate visual approaches. However, part of the training in the use of visual representations should focus on developing student independence in deciding which method to use.

Visual representations also are an excellent way for teachers to check what students already know about a topic and how well they understand the key relationships and issues. They can be used before, during, and after reading, and they are a useful study strategy that allows teachers to correct misunderstandings before formal assessment occurs. Furthermore, developing visual representations can become a cooperative learning activity, with small groups working together.

Story maps are graphic organizers with headings that are names of story elements, such as setting, problem, events, and resolution. These headings prompt students to locate key information from the story during or after reading, and write the information down. Research has shown that story maps help students develop a sense of story structure, which in turn improves their reading comprehension. Teachers first model story mapping by thinking aloud, locating information in the text, and writing down the information under the appropriate heading. The modeling process should include specific self-instruction statements, such as "As I read, I am finding and listing story elements so that I can understand what happens next," which helps students understand the purpose of the strategy and how to execute it (Swanson and De La Paz 1998).

Embedded Questions

If questions are embedded in a narrative or expository text, followed by blank lines where students can write or draw their answers, they help to interrupt ineffective reading processes and prompt students to actively work to comprehend a passage. Students might be asked to describe the setting, make a prediction, write a question, or summarize. Students also might mark up the text by highlighting evidence to support inferences, unfamiliar vocabulary, or words that establish the mood.

The embedded questions approach offers several benefits for learners: it gives students experience in annotating and manipulating text, promotes independent work with a text, and lays a foundation in comprehension that enables students to participate in substantive discussion of the reading. Furthermore, a carefully sequenced, guided implementation of embedded questions can increase students' awareness of metacognitive strategies and improve reading comprehension scores. Teachers could develop these exercises by copying Web-based text into a word processed document and then adding their own questions to it.

INSERT

INSERT was developed by Vaughn and Estes (1986) as a method for readers to recognize when their comprehension breaks down, and to encourage students to focus on new or important information within a text. It is particularly useful in situations where students own their books and are free to mark them. If this is not the case, students can simply attach post-it notes to the margins of their books. The instructor should write the following symbols on the board, and ask students to copy them:

Marking system for INSERT

X   I thought differently

+   New information

!   WOW

??   I don't understand

*   Very important

Allowing students to invent their own symbols is another technique that can be used to heighten interest in the approach and encourage its use.

Teacher Think-Alouds

One form of direct, explicit instruction in comprehension is the teacher think-aloud. In this technique, the teacher verbalizes how she or he makes sense of a text—for example, asking oneself questions, drawing on background knowledge, or stopping to reread. Salinger writes that think-alouds "externalize comprehension monitoring and give students models of behaviors they simply may not have acquired; this process gives them permission to not understand what they read the first time and ways to reread purposefully and productively. The goal of the think-aloud is to reveal the inner steps of reading for meaning" (2003, 83).

Strategies for Building Vocabulary

Vocabulary knowledge correlates strongly with reading comprehension (Hirsch 2003), and experts concur the best way to develop vocabulary is through wide reading. Hirsch (2003) points out that most vocabulary growth comes through immersion in reading. Therefore, approaches such as sustained silent reading and rich thematic studies are critical to vocabulary growth. Foil and Alber suggest:

> To develop a strong command of vocabulary and improve listening and reading comprehension, students must be provided with instruction that (a) facilitates linking new words to previous learning and background knowledge, (b) provides a personally meaningful context for using new words, and (c) presents frequent practice opportunities (2002, 138).

Some general tips for vocabulary instruction include:

- Model an interest in vocabulary, relating your own curiosity about words.

- Ask students to free-associate or brainstorm whatever comes to mind when they are presented with a new word. This approach helps teachers assess prior vocabulary knowledge and facilitate connections.

- Provide students with more than just a few brief exposures to truly learn new vocabulary. They need multiple opportunities to encounter the word in a variety of contexts, so that the word is internalized.

- Use techniques that actively involve students with new vocabulary words. Students need to see similarities and differences among words and consider multiple definitions and shades of meaning (Greenwood 2002).

Here are some specific strategies for helping students build vocabulary:

1) *The Vocabulary Self-Collection Strategy* (VSS) There are two varieties: the VSS for general vocabulary development, and the VSS for content-area vocabulary development.

   For general vocabulary development: Each student, as well as the teacher, brings to class a word that he or she believes the entire class should learn. Learners should look for words in their own environment—perhaps from their reading or even from a TV show they watched—and determine their meanings as best they can from context (they do not necessarily have to look up the word). Students share the word with the class, the class adds information to the definition, and then the entire class agrees on a definition with the teacher's guidance. A class word list is compiled by including student-selected words, excluding those words most students know and those that students choose not to learn at that time. At the end of the week, students are tested on the class word list.

   For content-area vocabulary development: The primary purpose in this case is to learn content, so students should be looking for words that will help them do so. After completing the assigned reading, students work in groups of two or three to identify words that are important for learning lesson content. The teacher then writes these words on the board, and student teams provide a definition from the context. Class members add any additional important information; the class then goes about creating a class word list, using the process described in the previous paragraph (Haggard 1986).

   In a study of usage of VSS by seventh- and eighth-graders, Ruddell and Shearer (2002) found that when students had the opportunity to select their own vocabulary words, they consistently chose important, challenging, interesting words. Also, students are more likely to learn their self-chosen words, remember the definitions over time, and put more effort into learning their own word lists versus commercially packaged lists.

2) *Facilitated Peer Dialogues* are another effective vocabulary building strategy. These dialogues occur in small discussion groups composed of two students, with the teacher nearby. The group meets once a reading assignment has been given. When one student encounters a word that is unfamiliar or confusing, he or she stops the reading and begins a discussion of the word's meaning. These discussions help students focus on word learning strategies and practice communication skills. They also provide the teacher with valuable assessment information, in terms of which strategies students use to figure out unknown words. Using this information, teachers can provide specific instruction in word learning strategies (Harmon 2002).

3) *Semantic Feature Analysis* is a technique that focuses attention on how words within a category are related. Steps include:

- Present students with a list of words that share a common feature.

- Ask students to list a characteristic, quality, or feature possessed by one of the words on the list. Put these words on the top of the board to create a matrix. Then ask students to fill in the matrix with pluses or minuses, to indicate whether each word has that quality or feature.

- When the matrix has been filled in and discussed, ask students to add more items (Greenwood 2002).

4) IT FITS

This strategy based on the use of keywords can provide struggling readers with critical support in vocabulary development. Students first write the word and its definition on an index card (**I**dentify the term and **T**ell the definition). Next, students **F**ind a keyword they know that will help them remember the vocabulary word and write it on the card. Then they **I**magine and **T**hink about a connection between the vocabulary word and the keyword, and draw a picture on the card to help them remember that connection. Finally, students **S**tudy the card until they have memorized the definition. For example, if the vocabulary word were "biomes" (large land areas where specific animals live), the student would write the word and its definition on the card. The student might select the keyword "homes" to remember this definition and write it down. To illustrate the connection between the words, the student might draw a nature scene where animals are enclosed in homes (Lebzelter and Nowacek 1999).

Strategies for Reading Internet Materials

Many middle and high school teachers have found valuable ways to incorporate the Internet into their curriculum. Too often, however, students' eagerness to work online is not matched with the kind of reflective, critical thinking that teachers expect them to do. Reading Internet text requires the same types of thinking skills as reading paper texts; however, its very nature poses some particular challenges. For example, it contains vast quantities of material that range widely in their accuracy. Also, Internet sources are continually changing, in contrast to the long shelf life of library books. Finally, the free-flowing nature of the Web as contrasted with textbooks can pose a particularly difficult challenge for students who lack effective reading strategies.

Therefore, students need instruction in determining the accuracy, authenticity, relevance, and point of view of the Web sites they visit. Also, the way in which some students are accustomed to navigating the Internet can be counterproductive to classroom research. As Burke points out, "Surfing invites typically impulsive adolescent students on a high-speed drive that allows no opportunities for reflection" (2002, 38). Before beginning an online search, students should:

- Ask themselves questions that help themselves set a goal or determine what type of information they are seeking.

- Anticipate which keywords will help them locate the information.

- Think about what criteria they will use for selecting documents to read. The criteria should be linked to the type of project. For example, if the student is preparing for a debate, he or she will look for persuasive documents in support of the argument; however, if the student is just beginning a research paper, he or she might be seeking recent news articles (Burke 2002).

Once students have located a promising site, they should ask themselves several questions that will help them evaluate the site's accuracy and point of view:

- Who is responsible for the content of the site?

- Who has authored the documents on the site?

- When were the documents last updated?

- Who is the intended audience? Any advertisements on the site may provide insight into this question.

- What other types of information are available on the site? This gives an overall idea of what types of information the site considers important.

- Does the site contain facts or opinions? If it contains facts, does it include references to back up its claims? If it contains opinions, does it include multiple points of view on a topic?

- Does the author identify and cite quoted material? (Burke 2002)

Peer Tutoring

Peer tutoring in reading has been shown to improve the reading skills of both the learner *and* the tutor. This strategy involves one student helping another student (or a small group of students) with lower academic skills, in a program structured and supervised by a teacher. Peer tutoring is a cost-effective way of dealing with the problem of too few teachers, and it also takes advantage of the power of peer influence.

Some other benefits of peer tutoring include:

- Tutees get individual attention they might not otherwise receive; they often identify better with peer tutors than with adult authority figures; and they receive immediate clarification of material they do not understand, in a nonthreatening environment that is optimally free of criticism and competition.

- Tutors get a chance to be leaders and assume responsibility, which helps build confidence and self-esteem. By explaining the subject matter to others, peer tutors come to understand it better themselves. In the view of Walberg and Paik, the "need to organize one's thoughts to impart them intelligibly to others, to become conscious of the value of time, and to learn managerial and social skills are probably the main reasons for benefits to the tutors" (2004, 33).

- Adolescents usually like tutoring because of its active and interactive nature.

- Teachers have more time to work with those most in need of assistance.

Many elements of reading can be incorporated into a peer tutoring program—word recognition, identifying story structure elements, and metacognitive skills such as text lookback (Rekrut 1994). Research suggests peer tutoring is most successful when teachers provide structured lesson plans for tutors to follow (Jenkins and Jenkins 1987), when specific skills are taught, and when responses are easily determined to be correct or incorrect (Miller et al. 1993).

Before taking on their roles as tutors, students should first be trained in interpersonal skills (helping without giving the answers, providing encouragement), as well as management skills (allocating time for tasks, measuring and recording student performance). Students should also be made aware of issues such as punctuality and confidentiality, as well as the purpose of the tutoring program itself.

Researchers suggest assigning tutors to same-sex partners for comfort and modeling reasons (Rekrut 1994). Tutors and tutees need not be in the same grade level; they are often several years apart in age, which is referred to as "cross-age tutoring." In the secondary school, students in the upper grades who have already successfully completed a class might tutor those in the lower grades. Another option is for secondary students to tutor elementary students; this activity is particularly well-suited to low-achieving secondary students, who can then review basic skills while being in a high-status role, and therefore will not perceive the task as "baby work" (Slavin 1986). One disadvantage of cross-age tutoring, however, is that it is not as easy to manage as regular peer tutoring, because it requires at least two teachers to organize the activity.

The Peer Assisted Learning Strategies Program

While not a tutoring program, PALS (Peer Assisted Learning Strategies) has some similarities with tutoring and been shown to be effective with high school students who have serious reading problems (Fuchs, Fuchs, and Kazdan 1999). The procedure involves three major activities:

1) *Partner Reading:* 10 minutes of sustained reading; higher-performing student reads first, followed by the lower-performing student rereading the same material. This is designed to improve accuracy and fluency.

2) *Paragraph Shrinking:* Continuing with the text, students read orally one paragraph at a time, stopping to identify the main idea. This is designed to develop comprehension through summarization.

3) *Prediction Relay*: Students formulate predictions about upcoming passage, and check their predictions after reading.

Researchers found that, when compared to a control group, those students who participated in PALS grew more on reading comprehension and reported more positive beliefs about working hard to improve their reading performance.

Some Things to Keep in Mind When Teaching Comprehension Strategies

Incorporating comprehension strategies into the curriculum involves more than teaching a set of techniques. While introducing strategies, teachers need to: emphasize the underlying purposes of using them, address obstacles students face when trying to learn them (such as ineffective techniques they may already be using), and actively promote strategy use (model it and link strategy use to learning outcomes).

One additional point is important. The National Reading Panel (2000) ana-lyzed 203 studies of comprehension strategy instruction. The Panel found that—in addition to teaching students individual strategies—they should be helped to use combinations of strategies. For example, embedded in reciprocal teaching are the strategies of summarization, question generation, and attention to vocabulary.

Make Sure Learners Understand a Strategy's Purpose

Comprehension strategies have the potential to increase students' reading skills, although educators must be aware that a strategy becomes a com-prehension tool only if its purpose is understood. For example, a student can only make good use of a visual representation strategy such as a web if he or she realizes that creating a web is a tool for thinking about and recording the relationships between different text elements. If the student

Steps to Teaching Learning Strategies

In their review of research on effective instructional practices, Walberg and Paik identify the teaching of learning strategies as a practice that "yields learning gains." They suggest that the teaching of learning strategies include:

- modeling, in which the teacher exhibits the desired behavior;

- opportunities for guided practice, in which students perform with help from the teacher; and

- application, in which students act independently of the teacher (2004, 32).

does not approach it with this in mind, the web is simply an assignment—an extra piece of busywork to complete. While efficient learners may implicitly know how to use comprehension approaches as tools, others may see no tie between approaches such as webbing and their efforts to learn content unless they receive special instruction.

Model the Use of a Strategy

When introducing specific comprehension strategies in the classroom, teachers should first model usage of the strategy. For example, a teacher might model prediction by thinking out loud: "The name of the chapter is Effects of Climate on Culture. I know that some places in the world are better for farming than others. Will this chapter talk about how communities in places like this are different from those that get almost no rain?" Bonds, Bonds, and Peach would describe this example as a "model of how one monitors, questions, and recalls what is to be learned" (1992, 56).

To facilitate student independence, teacher support should be gradually diminished. After the teacher provides several examples of thinking aloud while applying a strategy, students could take turns applying the strategy with help from the teacher and classmates, either in large or small groups. With this practice, students eventually will gain competence in performing the tasks independently (Curran 1997).

Link Strategy Use to Learning Outcomes

Holloway advises that middle and high school teachers must "constantly show remedial readers their progress . . . [and] how reading strategies are effective in improving their reading comprehension" (1999, 80).

Results from one study highlights the importance of motivation to strategic learning (Chan 1994). Findings indicate students who believe they have control over their learning outcomes and who have a positive image of their academic abilities are more likely to use strategies in their learning. The author asserts that the findings "support the need to provide students with strategy instruction and to convince them that learning outcomes are attributable to the use of strategies" (336). Teachers may find it useful to conduct an in-class demonstration that provides evidence that strategy use can improve learning.

Section Six

Assessment: Purposes and Approaches

Assessment of student learning can serve many purposes, and an understanding of these purposes can help teachers choose an appropriate assessment approach. For example, when evaluation includes the assignment of grades, teachers have a convenient vehicle for reporting student performance and progress to students, parents, and others. When a teacher provides comments and corrections, students receive valuable feedback that can improve future efforts. Additional purposes for reading assessment include:

1) *Highlighting assessment as a meaning-making process.* Approaches serving this purpose put a premium on engaging students in their reading materials and encouraging creativity, personal response, and interpretation. They have potential to promote better learning and a more in-depth understanding of subject matter.

2) *Providing teachers with diagnostic information on student reading level.* Approaches serving this purpose might be used to inform the instruction of students who have particular reading problems. Once a student's strengths and weaknesses have been identified, the instructor can determine which strategies might address the weaknesses.

Approaches That Highlight Assessment as a Meaning-Making Process

Book reports, quizzes, and short-answer tests are some of the traditional ways that a secondary school teacher might assess student understanding of assigned reading. These types of evaluation have come under criticism in recent years, however, because they fail to allow the reader to create meaning and respond to the text. Rather, they encourage the reader to passively recite or recall a reading's facts and details—which is likely to lose the interest and motivation of the typical adolescent reader. In addition, it is becoming increasingly clear that more actively involving students in self-assessment helps to engage them in learning.

As reading has come to be viewed as an interactive process that involves a transaction between reader and text, parallel evaluation methods have been developed. One example is portfolio assessment, in which students create portfolios of written work that include items such as their personal responses to reading assignments. The rationale behind these new types of assessment is that because reading is a dynamic process, it requires a dynamic form of assessment.

This is not to say that quizzes and standardized tests are without value altogether. There are certainly instances when a quiz can be useful, such as when a teacher needs a quick method of determining how much students have understood from a story. However, if used as the exclusive form of assessment, quizzes can have detrimental effects on learners. Because this form of assessment usually emphasizes recall of the plot itself and does not encourage students to engage in a more substantive analysis of a story, students trained in the "quiz habit" are likely to experience difficulty in subsequent writing assignments that call for in-depth interpretation (Johannessen 1994). This argument is supported by a case study of an English teacher who found that putting less emphasis on summaries of literature—coupled with the introduction of dialogue journals—resulted in the expression of more substantive ideas about literature, as seen in classroom discussion as well as in the student journals. The author of the study notes that "less emphasis on summary encouraged deeper analysis of reactions to specific characters and incidents, the very exploration of which necessitated incorporating the facts [the teacher] sought as reassurance that they had understood" (Gross 1992, 11).

In addition, a review of the research on classroom evaluation indicates dynamic types of assessment tend to promote better learning. The author concludes that classroom evaluation all too often emphasizes the importance of isolated pieces of information, when in fact information is remembered better and is often more useful when it is learned within a broader framework of meaningful interrelationships (Crooks 1988).

Two basic goals of dynamic reading instruction are heightening student engagement and instilling in students a love of reading. However, these goals may appear to be incompatible with an approach that always holds students accountable for what they read. One possible remedy for this dilemma is to provide time for assessment-free independent reading during the school day (see page 29). This is not to suggest that assessment should be eliminated entirely; rather, the trick is to find ways to turn the assessment process itself into something that excites students about reading, encourages them to develop their own understandings of a text, and provides information that can be used to improve the instructional process.

The new emphasis on assessment as a meaning-making process stands in sharp contrast to the traditional definition of assessment as something produced after the learning has occurred, in order to measure what has been learned. In fact, assessment should be part of the learning process, not separate from it. Learning can occur *while* students are creating something that will be assessed, as well as once they receive teacher feedback on the product they have created.

Although assessment methods that emphasize student meaning-making— such as essay writing, portfolios, and personal anthologies—may seem more relevant for English classes than for content-area classes, most can be easily adapted for content-area assignments. For example, portfolios are now being used in math classes; these portfolios might include student-formulated problems or samples of journal writing related to mathematical concepts being studied (Crowley 1993).

Teachers who implement these methods will need to be aware that they may have to spend more time evaluating and providing feedback on student work. It will probably take longer to grade a personal response essay than a short-answer test about the plot of a story. At the same time, learners will need to increase their time investment as well, as they are called upon to make more thoughtful interpretations and responses to a text.

Essays

Essay writing is an integral part of assessment in the English classroom, and is frequently used in the content-area classroom as well. Findings of a national study of high school literature programs underscore the value of essay writing as a learning tool. This study found that English teachers in award-winning schools placed more emphasis on essays than did those in other schools (Applebee 1993).

The nature of essay assignments can vary widely. An essay assignment might call for formal analysis of a text only, or it might also call upon the reader to include a personal response. The referenced national study found that text-based essays are assigned far more often than essays that stress a reader's personal response or interpretation (Applebee 1993). However, personal response-oriented essays have been found to be comparable to text-based essays in their effects on the understanding of literary texts (Marshall 1987). In Marshall's study, personal response-oriented essay assignments asked students to explain and elaborate upon their responses to a story, drawing on their own values and experiences to make sense of their reactions to the text.

When the researchers interviewed these students, they found that they sometimes perceived formal analytic writing as merely an exercise, while personal essays provided an opportunity to begin the process of independent analysis.

Portfolios

A portfolio is a collection of formal and informal student work, connected to what has been read and studied, that reveals student progress. Portfolio items range from self-assessments to teacher observations, attitude and interest surveys, writing samples (both complete and in-progress), evidence that the student reads for enjoyment and information, retellings, summaries, responses to readings, and journal entries. Portfolios have been criticized for not providing measures of overall student progress similar to those provided by large-scale assessments, as well as for low interrater reliability (the consistency with which different readers assign the same score to a single portfolio). However, portfolios do show promise as tools for assessing individual student progress and for encouraging teachers to change their instructional approaches in the direction of more active student involvement (Viadero 1995).

Portfolios encourage student involvement in two important ways. First, they call on each student to document and reflect upon his or her own progress. Second, while students compile portfolios, they decide which works to include and why. This process of selection—again, with the help of teacher modeling—can foster the development of personal criteria against which a student can judge quality and effort, thereby encouraging future efforts to improve.

Personal Anthologies

Developing a personal anthology can motivate learners to read widely and make connections between the different works they read. The advantage of this assignment is that, while it calls upon students to create a finished product for evaluation, it highlights the reading activity itself as something that is enjoyable and personally meaningful. Students create a personal anthology by acting as editor: they search for works of literature that best connect with their interests and tastes, develop a theme, and then compile these works into an anthology (Sullivan 1988).

Sullivan advises teachers to instruct students that, as they compile their personal anthologies, they should read only works that interest them, and put away anything they find boring. The theme of a personal anthology should be entirely student selected, so students focus on those interests or ideas that have greatest personal meaning to them. Sullivan writes, "The connection with self explains the almost fierce sense of pride and ownership that my students feel about their anthologies" (1988, 28). Anthologies developed by students could also form the basis for future work or reading by other students. The product of assessment can thus be applied to different purposes.

Although students are allowed a great deal of choice, the teacher should be precise about certain requirements. For example, directions should be given about general types of literature to be read. The teacher might require specific numbers of poems, essays, and works of short fiction—all divided among different genres, such as science fiction, works by Southern writers, and works by fellow students. Teachers should also develop stringent guidelines as to the actual preparation of the anthology. Sullivan recommends requiring elements such as a title page, a table of contents, a preface with opinions about the works chosen and why they were chosen, and a bibliography. The anthology could be evaluated by assigning each element a maximum number of points, and adding the points in each category to arrive at a total score.

Other Alternative Evaluation Methods

A number of other ideas are listed below. These are all appropriate for language arts assessment (that is, when evaluating students' understanding of a story), and could also be applied in the content areas, such as when studying historically significant events or people relating to that particular subject area.

- *Continuation of a story*. Have students continue the plot after the end of the story, by describing what happens to the main character.

- *Point of view*. Have students rewrite the material from the point of view of another character who was not a narrator.

- *Rewrite the ending.* Students often have their own ideas about how a story, either fiction or nonfiction, should have ended. Rewriting can be done individually or by groups creating scripts; the scripts can then be acted out for the rest of the class.

- *Newspapers.* Students can write newspaper articles about an event or several events in the text or historical occurrence. These can be interviews, feature articles, or photo essays.

- *Literary panel.* Students can play the roles of characters from a story or historical event. They form a panel and are interviewed about the parts they play.

- *Relating material to themselves.* For example, if a class reads *Huckleberry Finn*, students could write a modern-day version of the novel, casting themselves as Huck, describing their journeys and struggles. Alternatively, if a science class were reading about efforts to develop a polio vaccine, they might compare this with how they feel about the efforts to find a cure for AIDS.

- *Paradigms.* A paradigm can be a graphic display on posterboard, in which students relate their hobbies and interests to the elements of the written material. For example, one student diagrammed the opposing themes of depression and resurrection in *The Grapes of Wrath* across a basketball court; another illustrated and explained the novel's rising and falling action by depicting a surfer approaching waves (Guzzetti 1990).

- *Scripting a meeting of characters.* Students can be asked to imagine that four of the characters from the materials they have read have gathered in one place. Working in small groups, they imagine what would happen and create a script. They perform the script in front of classmates, and then write reflective essays on their experience working on this project (Tuley 1994).

- *Other methods* of evaluation include creating drawings of the main characters, rewriting the text as a play or poem, and developing book covers, collages, and games.

Student projects should be evaluated on the basis of how consistent they are with the material presented, and on whether they have considered relevant concepts, issues, and events. Naturally, some forms of evaluation will work better with some material than others. For example, a story or historical event with a controversial ending would be particularly appropriate for an assignment to rewrite the ending.

Approaches Designed to Provide Teachers with Information on Student Reading Level

When working with students whose reading deficiencies significantly interfere with their attention to the material, teachers may need to use specific techniques to assess the nature of the problems. Gathering information on student reading level allows educators to identify students' specific strengths and weaknesses in terms of reading comprehension abilities, identify teaching strategies that target the weak areas, and decide which kinds of reading strategies students need to practice. Several methods of gathering information are discussed in the following pages: teacher observation, the Cloze procedure, retellings, miscue analysis, and informal reading inventories.

Many of these methods are used routinely by reading specialists, and are used less often by content-area teachers and English teachers; for example, most reading specialists have received special training in the technique of miscue analysis. Other techniques, such as teacher observation and retellings, are more familiar to teachers. The purpose of this section is to provide an overview of some different diagnostic tools, in order to inform teachers of the kinds of steps that might be taken with students who have reading difficulties—even if the teachers will not actually be implementing actions suggested by the diagnosis. Some of these tools also could be used by subject-area teachers, perhaps in collaboration with the reading specialist. When teachers do not have reading specialists available, they will need additional administrative support for their own efforts to learn about and use diagnostic tools.

Gathering this kind of diagnostic information can be an important tool for teachers, providing information on reading level and reading progress that can help to inform instruction, as well as providing material for subsequent graded assessment and other feedback teachers give students about their performance. Diagnostic tools need not be used with all students all the time. They are often most effectively employed when a teacher is concerned about a particular student who is having difficulty with the information presented in the written materials.

Teacher Observation

Perhaps the most reliable and useful information about reading level can be gained by the observations teachers make on a day-to-day basis. These observations can provide a more accurate and complete picture than the snapshot provided by a reading test. Teachers might record their observations about individual students, either in a notebook or on a form or checklist. Because of the time required for tracking all students with notebook comments, teachers may choose instead to write about the progress of just a few students who are especially in need of assistance.

Teachers might also record their observations on a form that provides space for brief comments about each student, or check off skills and behaviors from a checklist. These tools are designed to record general reading skills or specific behaviors, such as comprehension, motivation and interest, and vocabulary usage. Because the space for recording is small, it encourages brief comments that do not require a great deal of time.

Cloze Procedure

This is a useful, time-efficient procedure for determining reading level, and it also can be used for assessing the readability of classroom reading material. The Cloze procedure requires several steps (Cheek 1992):

1) Select a passage of approximately 300 words.

2) Use a formula to determine readability (see pages 87-89).

3) Retype the passage leaving the first and last sentences intact, but delete every fifth word.

4) Type an underline to replace the omitted words (all underlines should be of the same length).

5) Instruct students to fill in the blanks with the words that best complete the sentences.

6) Score student responses, counting words that make sense as correct. Criteria: more than 60 percent correct is "independent" reading level, 40 percent to 60 percent correct is "instructional" reading level, and below 40 percent correct is "frustration" reading level.

Retellings

The retelling technique involves giving students time to read a passage, perhaps also allowing for time to take notes or to rehearse information, and then asking them to write a retelling without referring to the original passage. This technique gives the teacher insight into student comprehension processes, such as *how* information is organized into a whole and *how much* information is gained from the passage.

Miscue Analysis

This technique, developed from the research of Kenneth and Yetta Goodman, involves examining the oral reading performance of learners. The word *miscue* refers to an instance when the reader reads something that is different from the printed text. This approach does not involve an exact scoring of reading level, but rather a qualitative analysis of the reader's strengths and weaknesses, based on the student's oral reading of a passage and retelling of it.

Informal Reading Inventories

Informal reading inventories (IRIs) are often constructed by the teacher or the reading specialist. They are also sometimes found in basals. The benefit of a teacher-constructed IRI is that it is tailored to the materials in the specific instructional program, because it typically uses a sampling of curricular materials. Also, teachers can devise an IRI that will highlight the constructive nature of reading, as evidenced by the following example.

Brozo (1990) developed an IRI that emphasizes that a student's ability to comprehend is not fixed or constant, but varies across tasks and settings and is influenced by a variety of factors, such as prior knowledge and interest. Components include:

1) *Diagnostic interview.* Teacher first collects information about students' reading attitudes and reading interests, which reading strategies they use, any background information they have about the topic, and their awareness of the goals and purposes of reading.

2) *Preparing to read.* Teacher builds motivation for reading the passage by activating background knowledge, setting purposes for reading, and preteaching important vocabulary and concepts.

3) *Reading silently.* This allows students to work through miscues on their own and to identify unknown words before reading out loud.

4) *During oral reading.* At this time, the teacher should model comprehension processes with self-questioning and by thinking out loud. Students give self-reports on their own comprehension strategies.

5) *After reading.* Students generate retellings. The teacher uses the retellings to assess comprehension and then extend student understanding of the passage with discussion.

Section Seven

Issues Specific to Content-Area Reading

Many issues, ideas, and suggestions described earlier are relevant to—and in some cases, critical for—content-area reading instruction. This section, however, focuses on issues specific to content reading.

First, three of the core content areas (social studies, science, and math) are examined individually in terms of the special reading skills they demand and the techniques that might develop these skills. Next, approaches for using literature in content-area classrooms are described. Another concern that is addressed is textbook usage and ways in which content teachers might use textbooks most effectively. Implicit in the discussion of these issues is this position expressed by Barton, "Making literacy a top priority means reading skills must be incorporated into courses across the curriculum throughout the middle school and high school years" (1997, 23).

Reading Skills Needed in Some Specific Content Areas

There is great variety among the content areas in terms of demands placed on the reader. It stands to reason, for example, that the reading skills needed in math class differ sharply from those required for reading in social studies. The focus here is on three of the core content areas—mathematics, science, and social studies—as examples of how reading skills and reading instruction can be integrated into content areas. In addition to helping students achieve greater mastery in the specific content area discussed, many of the reading skills can also be applied to other situations.

Reading in Social Studies

Social studies demands not only basic skills such as recall of details, sequence of events, and recognition of main ideas, but also a higher level of critical thinking, involving interpretation, synthesis, and analysis. Cochran writes that the challenge to social studies students is to master facts, and then "think about how these facts contributed to the events of the past as well as how they can be used to predict future events" (1993, 3). Two important critical reading skills are recognizing cause-and-effect relationships and distinguishing fact from opinion.

Teachers can help students recognize cause-and-effect relationships by:

- Presenting real-life examples.

- Calling attention to signal words in expository writing. Signal words include "because," "therefore," "so," and "in order to." Have students find examples of these words in their textbook.

- Elaborating on cause-and-effect situations during the school day. For example, ask students: "What would happen if you didn't turn in your homework? Why would that happen?" (Hickey 1990).

Some techniques teachers can use to assist students in developing the ability to distinguish fact from opinion include:

- Asking students to analyze newspaper articles, examine the statements presented in them, and determine which ones are verifiable facts.

- Having students restate factual information as opinion, and opinion as fact.

- Dividing the class into pairs, with each pair given a list of names, events, and terminology related to a current social studies topic. One partner compiles a list of facts related to the topic, while the other collects opinions. Students then work in groups of four, where each pair takes turns reading one of its statements and asking the other pair whether the statement is fact or opinion (Hickey 1990).

Other crucial skills in social studies reading include identifying propaganda techniques, identifying the author's purpose (including obvious public purposes and possible "hidden" purposes), and recognizing bias and emotionally charged words. In order to motivate students to develop some of these skills, a teacher could provide students with two or more accounts of an historical event, or even newspaper accounts of a current event. Students would then be asked to compare and contrast the authors' points of view, accuracy, and use of bias or persuasive language.

The PEP Road Map strategy (Katims and Harmon 2000) helps at-risk students learn material from social studies textbooks. Low-achieving readers often do not engage in self-talk to make sense of the social studies texts they are reading, so the strategy is founded on first asking the question: Will I be reading about a **P**erson, **E**vent, or **P**lace.

The students then use a series of PEP questions as a guide, taking notes to answer the questions. (Sample questions are determined by whether the passage is about a person, event, or place, and might include: What happened? When and where? Important words? What did he or she do?) After taking notes on the PEP questions, the next step is for the students to turn their notes into guiding questions that will help peers who are reading the same passage. The researchers found middle school students who used this strategy improved their reading comprehension, metacognitive ability, attention to information in texts, and confidence in ability to grapple with ideas in authentic texts.

Another strategy for working with social studies texts is Questioning the Author (Beck and McKeown 2002). This strategy calls on students to grapple with ideas as they read. Rather than a traditional emphasis on learning facts from a text, the focus of this strategy is to build meaning and evaluate the author's ability to communicate ideas. At certain points within the text, teachers insert queries that are based on goals for student understanding. Questions typically focus on asking about what an author's statement means, what the author is telling the audience, or how an author's statement fits in with what students have already learned about a topic.

Reading in Science

Science reading materials are often particularly challenging for students with reading difficulties. This is because these materials are typically characterized by an expository style, terse and exact wording, and an abundance of technical vocabulary, symbols, and formulas. Comprehension of scientific materials can be enhanced, however, by using many of the techniques previously mentioned, such as comprehension strategies, cooperative learning groups, vocabulary development methods, and supplementing the textbook with materials such as scientific articles in popular magazines or profiles of famous scientists. Science teachers also can make use of analogies in order to help students make connections between the abstract concepts they read about and their previous experience. Another technique that promotes greater conceptual understanding is asking students to make predictions and discuss ideas when they are just beginning to learn about a scientific concept.

Science involves tasks such as finding solutions to problems, gathering data, conducting experiments, and interpreting results. For this reason, science teachers should emphasize reading skills such as following directions and drawing conclusions. Also essential are problem-solving skills: defining the problem, looking at it thoroughly, and then organizing a plan of attack for solving it. Moreover, science teachers should encourage students to be risk takers when they read, considering more than one possible solution to a problem (Cochran 1993).

"Science anxiety" is a term that has spawned a great deal of discussion in recent years. Educators are concerned about many students' low level of success in science, and their avoidance of studying it whenever possible (Mallow 1991). Many students perceive science as a field suited for only the most intellectual, a field too difficult for them to understand. A legitimate goal for science teachers, then, should be to raise students' awareness of science as an approach for investigating everyday problems, as well as those beyond our comprehension (Cochran 1993). By using articles about scientific current events or materials about people who have chosen a career in science, science teachers may help students to see the applicability of science to real life, as well as broadening the types of science reading materials available for use in the classroom.

Teachers can support learning of science vocabulary and concepts in several ways. Hands-on science activities—such as conducting experiments and gathering data—provide teachers with an opportunity to use content-area vocabulary words in a relevant context. This approach will help students understand vocabulary words more deeply. For example, learning the meaning of the word *permeable* is easier and more meaningful if the word is used in the context of a relevant lab experiment (Barton 1997).

One middle school teacher introduced the following types of activities to help students with reading and learning science material:

- *Sequencing activities.* Teach students to identify the object, procedure, or initiating event; then explain the stages or series that follow, showing how one leads to the next; and then describe the outcome.

For example, students were asked to retrace the steps of a lost hamster or to consider what would happen if earthworms were set free. Students described the sequence in a creative writing piece.

- *Cause/effect activities.* To promote critical thinking, the science teacher came up with a twist: he presented written effects and asked the students to brainstorm the causes.

- *The RAFT technique.* The teacher asked the students to take on the role of a living or nonliving thing, and then to think from its perspective. There are four components to this procedure: the **R**ole (such as a scientist, a tulip tree, the element oxygen); the **A**udience to whom the piece is addressed (such as a squirrel or a drop of water); the **F**ormat (e.g., a letter, a comic strip, a skit, or a poem); and the **T**opic (such as a letter to a predator asking why it preys on you, or a skit that describes a day in the life of a tree) (Loranger 1999).

Reading in Mathematics

Math texts are like science texts in that they include many symbols and are written compactly. Yet, math texts are unique reading materials in several important ways. For example, they include a large amount of nonverbal material and therefore require slow and deliberate reading for comprehension. In addition, mathematicians take common words and add technical definitions to them—such as the word *and*, which usually means *plus* when used in math problems.

Another unique aspect of mathematical reading is that, in the case of equations, each number or symbol and its position on the page relative to others is especially important. In the case of word problems, the order of the words, as well as the functional relation between words, are crucial to the text's meaning. Word problems are made more challenging by the fact that different components are linked together by prepositions; students reading these problems may need special instruction in preposition usage. Also, the students reading these problems often are not aware that analytical reading is necessary, and they may lack experience and skill in this kind of reading (MacGregor 1990).

Strategies for teaching reading in math include:

- When presenting students with word problems, ask them for definitions of key terms and interpretations of important phrases.

- Ask students to rephrase a complicated word problem in their own words, perhaps breaking the problem down into a series of simple sentences.

- Provide direct instruction in reading math textbooks in terms of four factors: terminology (identifying and learning the terms needed for the problem on which the student is working), eye patterns (reading math expressions involving parentheses from the inside and moving outward), graph/text interaction (stopping at intermediate stages of a sample problem to identify patterns emerging on a graph), and reading direction (sometimes starting from the final step of the solution rather than reading problems from top to bottom) (Ostler 1997).

- Use the chalkboard and the overhead projector to help students with their reading. Visually represent the material and encourage a discussion of mathematical symbols and terms (Cochran 1993).

- Model and allow students to practice translating mathematical word sentences to symbols, and equations to words; the translation can be written directly underneath the original expression to illustrate the correspondence (Fuentes 1998).

- Use the technique of thinking out loud in order to model how one might interpret a problem and go about solving it.

- Increase interest and motivation for reading mathematical language by encouraging recreational reading of materials with high math content, such as earned run averages in baseball and statistical information from surveys (Fuentes 1998).

- Ask students to keep a math journal, writing out definitions or exploring concepts.

- Implement post-reading discussions in math class about topics such as: new or familiar ideas in the reading, real-world applications the concepts might have, and the steps the author recommended following versus the steps students actually used (Tanner and Casados 1998).

To reinforce what was stated earlier, many of the approaches—while especially helpful for improving learning in a particular content area—provide the student with reading-related skills generalizable to other settings.

For example, an understanding of cause-and-effect relationships discussed in the section on social studies is not only important in social studies, but is also essential in the fields of mathematics and science, as well as in everyday life.

Using Literature in the Content-Area Classroom

High-quality literature is not the exclusive domain of English classes: when integrated into other content-area courses, it can more fully develop ideas and concepts than a textbook alone. Many high-quality picture books are appealing to all age groups and offer a wealth of information. For example, the *Eyewitness Readers* series explains abstract concepts in science and math through models and diagrams. Narrative picture books such as David Macauley's *Cathedral* and Maruki's *Hiroshima No Pika* provide rich detail on historical sites or events (Vacca and Vacca 1993). Spicer suggests that the artwork included in children's picture books such as *The Librarian Who Measured the Earth* or *Sir Cumference and the Dragon of Pi* "can make mathematics concepts real for [high school] students" (2003, 5).

In their book *Content Area Reading*, Vacca and Vacca write:

> Fiction entices readers to interact with texts from a number of perspectives that are impossible to achieve in nonfiction alone. Fantasy, traditional (e.g., folktales and myths), historical, and realistic fiction, for example, help readers to step outside of their actual worlds for a while to consider a subject from a different point of view. And by doing so, they learn something about what it means to be a human being on this planet of ours (1993, 301).

Because of the variety of topics found in trade books for adolescent readers, they lend themselves to interdisciplinary connections. Pottle (1996) offers the following guidelines for finding trade books that provide the strongest across-the-curriculum connections:

1) Are the book's characters believable? That is, do they act and react as real people do?

2) Do the characters change during the course of the book?

3) By reading this book, will students learn more about a scientific concept and its practical application?

4) Are the statements presented as facts accurate?

5) Is the novel set in a specific time period? Is this time period represented realistically?

6) Has the book been prepared with care? Is the illustration on the cover eye-catching? Is the print clear and easily read? If there are illustrations, do they enhance the text?

Using Textbooks

Allington (2002) writes that many students who have been making adequate progress in reading stumble in fourth grade, when the textbook typically becomes the primary reading source. This occurs because the vocabulary is less conversational and familiar, has more specialized terms and abstract ideas, contains more complex syntax, and has a greater emphasis on inferential thinking and prior knowledge. Flanagan agrees with Allington's concern about over-reliance on textbooks. In her view:

> Poor readers expend much energy and time struggling with individual words rather than constructing meaning from the text…. [In addition,] many textbooks are organized so that main ideas are embedded and too many concepts are treated superficially (1996, online).

"In an effort to make an overwhelming amount of information manageable and the content more accessible, textbook editors and nonfiction writers use various text structures. Yet for many students, especially average and struggling students, these structures are invisible. Think of this problem as the difference between trying to find a knife in a junk drawer versus trying to find a knife in an organized silverware drawer. To the student who can't see text structure, every text looks like a junk drawer" (Strong et al. 2002, 6-7)

Many students who fall behind at this point will never recover, unless they are given more instructional support. Although a 95-97 percent accuracy level has been considered appropriate for textbooks, Allington suggests educators might want to consider purchasing easier-to-read textbooks—ones students can read independently with 98-99 percent accuracy—and which allow them to better focus on content.

Ciborowski (1992) contends good textbooks meet four broad criteria:

1) They include pre-reading strategies that connect learning to student experience, thereby igniting student interest.

2) They emphasize the importance of teaching comprehension and thinking skills as well as content.

3) They describe novel assessment practices that will give teachers ideas for helping students consolidate new textbook knowledge with existing knowledge.

4) They are written in a style that is both engaging and well-organized.

Even textbooks that meet these criteria, however, can be too difficult for some students whose reading skills are far below grade level.

Readability and Readability Formulas

Educators should learn how to determine the readability level of a textbook for two purposes:

1) Individual teachers might have the opportunity to assist with textbook selection.

2) Once the textbook is in use, teachers want to determine whether certain parts of it (or the entire book) are appropriate for the reading level of their students.

What teachers learn about the readability level of the textbook will guide decisions about adapting the material for their students.

A variety of *readability formulas* exist. Their purpose is twofold: to help publishers develop texts that are at the reading level for which they were intended; and to help educators determine the reading level of instructional materials. Most readability formulas are based on average sentence length and complexity of words within several sample passages from a text. For example, one widely used formula, the Fry Readability Graph, requires the random selection of three passages within a text. By counting out 100 words and then counting the number of sentences and syllables within the 100 words, an average sentence length and average number of syllables can be obtained. These numbers are then plotted on a graph designed for estimating readability, and the area in which the plotted point falls gives the approximate grade level.

Other readability formulas include the Flesch Reading Ease Formula, the McLaughlin SMOG Index, Klesch-Kincaid Reading Level, and the Dale-Chall Formula.

Readability Analysis Resources

- Microsoft Word includes a tool that can calculate the Klesch-Kincaid Reading Level of text that can be opened in Word or that is copied and pasted into a Word document. Under Tools, select Spelling and Grammar, select Options, then Show Readability Statistics. After Word has finished checking spelling, information about the grade level of the text will be provided.

- Information on how to use the Fry approach and a PDF document, the Fry Readability Graph, can be found at http://school.discovery.com/schrockguide/fry/fry.html.

While readability formulas can provide valuable information about a text, they do not consider some of the most important student factors that determine readability, such as prior knowledge and motivation. In addition, they do not take into account textual features such as text clarity, chapter titles, paragraph divisions, subtitles, and illustrations—all of which can improve readability.

One alternate technique that does take the above factors into account is the FLIP framework (Schumm and Mangrum 1991). This technique calls upon the students to evaluate the difficulty of reading material. It is grounded in the principle that readers first need to have an idea of the difficulty of a task before they can plan how to approach it.

FLIP stands for **F**riendliness, **L**anguage, **I**nterest, and **P**rior knowledge; students are asked to flip through the text and look for those four factors. Specifically, the factors call upon students to evaluate the text in the following ways:

- *Friendliness*. Does the assignment contain "friendly elements" such as a table of contents, headings, and a glossary?

- *Language*. How difficult is the language? (What is the vocabulary level; how complicated are the sentences?)

- *Interest*. How interesting is my reading assignment? (Look at the title, introduction, headings, summary, pictures, and graphics, and rate how interesting the assignment is based on these factors.)

- *Prior knowledge*. What do I already know about the topic?

Students add the ratings they give each of the four elements and determine whether the level of the assignment is "comfortable," "somewhat comfortable," or "uncomfortable." They then determine an appropriate reading rate and budget their reading or study time. Students using the FLIP framework were found to make more realistic predictions about estimated reading/study time and to improve their test performance.

Adapting Textbooks That Are in Use

Once the reading level of a text is assessed, the text may require adaptation to accommodate various reading levels. Adaptation becomes even more crucial in the upper grades for two reasons: multilevel texts for content-area courses are available less often, and students in the upper grades vary more than younger students in terms of their reading levels. Research suggests the reading ability range within an age group is equal to two-thirds of the chronological age. For example, while students in a fourth-grade class might be as much as three grade levels lower or higher than average fourth-grade reading level, students in a 10th-grade class might be as much as *five* grade levels lower or higher than the average 10th-grade reading level. This increased range in reading ability in the upper grades accentuates the importance of adapting a textbook when it is too hard for some students to read. Furthermore, adapting a textbook by supplementing it with diverse sources of information, including movies and works of literature, will enhance student interest.

According to one study (Schumm, Vaughn, and Saumell 1992), middle and high school students did not feel they were being exposed to the kinds of instructional adaptations that would help them understand the textbook. These students endorsed the following suggestions for dealing with a textbook that is hard to understand:

- *Rewrite content material.* This can be done either by teachers or students. Teachers can tailor difficult material to the reading level of students; students who understand the text can rewrite it for peers who do not understand.

- *Supplement textbooks with other textbooks written at a lower level.* Some textbooks are published in multilevel versions. That is, two different versions of a textbook may appear the same and may cover the same material page for page, but the material within the books differs in terms of readability level.

- *Supplement textbooks with trade books or with Web-based materials.* This exposes students to a number of different kinds of contact with concepts and enhances comprehension.

- *Create in-class vertical files.* These are teacher-created (or student-created) files of materials, such as magazine or newspaper articles, relating to specific topics. Up-to-date information makes students aware of the relevance of the subject to their own lives.

- *Use audiovisual aids.* These might include films, audiotapes, television, and pictures.

One caution: those who rewrite textbooks (either publishers who are trying to attain a certain readability score or teachers who want to make difficult material more understandable for their students) run the risk of oversimplifying concepts and taking out important words in their efforts to shorten texts. When sentences are shortened to conform to readability formulas, important words such as *however*, *because*, and *in addition to* may be deleted, and the writing then becomes stilted, dull, and less coherent (Ciborowski 1992).

A study of eighth-grade readers demonstrates that both less-able readers and able readers gain more vocabulary knowledge from reading an *elaborated* text than from reading a simpler, revised text (Herman et al. 1987). The authors note: "Texts will not necessarily be made easier by making them short and superficial. What is critical is that they convey important information precisely, with interconnections fully explained at a level of specificity appropriate for readers who do not know much about the subject matter" (281).

Section Eight

Schoolwide Support for Literacy Instruction

Many middle schools and high schools have introduced a variety of quick-fix reading and writing programs, only to see them fall far short of the anticipated results. Such schools may benefit from adoption of a fundamentally new and more comprehensive approach. To help school leaders with this task, the Educational Alliance at Brown University has developed the Adolescent Literacy Support Framework, a "diagnostic tool to help school leaders identify how to initiate improvement" (2003, online).

This framework includes four key components: student motivation, research-based literacy strategies for teaching and learning, support for reading and writing across the curriculum, and organizational structures and leadership that ensure support, sustainability, and focus.

This last component—schoolwide leadership and organizational structures that sustain literacy initiatives—provides a strong foundation on which the other three components are built. The organizational structure and leadership capacity supports the literacy framework by:

- meeting agreed-upon goals for adolescents in that particular community;

- articulating, communicating, and actualizing literacy as a priority;

- implementing best practices for systemic educational reform;

- defining the literacy initiative in concert with the larger educational program;

- providing ongoing support for teacher professional development (see pages 100-101 for more information on this); and

- establishing a clear process for program evaluation (Meltzer and Okashige 2001).

More information about the Adolescent Literacy Support Framework can be found on the Knowledge Loom at http://www.knowledgeloom.org.

Brozo and Hargis describe the efforts of one high school faculty to "make reading more responsive to all students" (2003, 14). As a first step, an intensive assessment process was implemented in order to develop information on the reading ability of each student. In one 10th-grade class, the assessment process identified a "staggering 15-grade-level spread . . . 9 out of 24 students had reading levels at the 8th grade or below; 7 were within the 9th- to 10th-grade interval; and 8 had scores from the 11th-grade to nearly the 19th-grade level" (14).

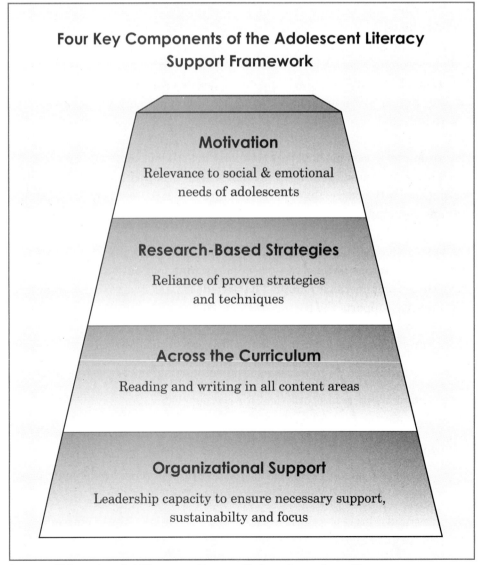

Four Key Components of the Adolescent Literacy Support Framework

Motivation

Relevance to social & emotional needs of adolescents

Research-Based Strategies

Reliance of proven strategies and techniques

Across the Curriculum

Reading and writing in all content areas

Organizational Support

Leadership capacity to ensure necessary support, sustainabilty and focus

Source: Educational Alliance at Brown University n.d., online.

After discussing the data, the school staff decided to implement four approaches designed to ensure that needs of both low- and high-performing students—as well as those reading on grade level—were better met. These initiatives included:

- opportunities for sustained silent reading;

- reading of young adult novels in the content classroom;

- provision of alternatives to the textbook for both struggling and superior readers; and

- a "Reading Buddy" program for students who had very low scores on the achievement tests.

When students were assessed again in mid-May, there was significant improvement, with nearly half the students increasing their scores by two or more grade levels. Teachers also observed that students who had previously had problems with reading participated more actively in class and made greater efforts to read.

Riggs and Gil-Garcia talk about the strength of taking a schoolwide approach to teaching learning/comprehension strategies:

> A schoolwide approach allows a scope and sequence to be established, with teachers at different grade levels and in different subject areas responsible for instructing students how to use specific skills. [In addition,] students can be encouraged to practice and generalize their new skills across classes.... Schoolwide support will help teachers to feel more comfortable spending class time on such instruction instead of focusing exclusively on teaching content standards required by the state or district.... Finally, teachers need support in their efforts to learn about and incorporate strategy training in their subject-area instruction. A schoolwide approach provides a natural platform for appropriate professional development and a forum in which teachers can share experiences and learn from each other (2001, 72-73).

Schoolwide Approaches—Some Examples

A variety of schoolwide approaches to adolescent literacy—or support programs designed to be implemented schoolwide—have been developed. Descriptions of a few of these follow.

Ramp-Up to Advanced Literacy Course

The National Center on Education and the Economy (NCEE) has developed a detailed framework for literacy instruction, its Ramp-Up to Advanced Literacy Course, which recently has been field-tested in secondary schools (Codding 2001). This program is a reading and writing workshop designed for delivery during a 90-minute, double-block period five days a week over the entire school year. The workshop has four parts:

1) Reading Instruction Block, during which the teacher closely observes students as they read one-on-one or in small-group settings;

2) Independent Reading Block, during which students spend 10 to 20 minutes reading a self-selected book independently;

3) Read-Aloud Block, during which a teacher thinks aloud as she reads, to demonstrate her reading strategies and processes; and

4) Project Unit Block, during which students undertake author and genre studies. This block often involves the writing of students' own books, which are then shared with others.

The social aspect of learning is critical to this program: teachers model good reading behaviors; students collaborate on projects, read together, or discuss literature; and opportunities for cross-age tutoring are provided, as students explore children's storybooks and share them with younger children.

Reciprocal Reading

Weedman and Weedman discuss the schoolwide introduction of Reciprocal Reading, a program designed for struggling high school readers, in a Kentucky high school. The program teaches students to anticipate and formulate questions about text. They learn how to "ask questions while they read and, as they become better readers, to make meaning from text inferences and their prior knowledge of the subject" (2001, 43).

Teachers were trained to use the process, which begins with 20 to 30 minutes spent each day for eight days on "instructing students how to generate factual questions, summarize, clarify meaning and intent, and predict" (2001, 44). This was followed by opportunities for guided practice and then for group sharing. The instruction was provided in every classroom. Weedman and

Weedman report students improved substantially in their ability to answer both factual and inference questions.

Strategic Reading

Another program, Strategic Reading, is actually an instructional component of the Talent Development High Schools. The course is designed for ninth-grade students whose reading levels are more than two years below grade level. Students served by the program are given a "double dose" of English in two 18-week terms of 90-minute classes. In the first term students follow the Strategic Reading curriculum, an approach that uses high-interest materials with a readability level appropriate for participants and that focuses on fluency and comprehension skills. During the second 18-week term, students use the district's English syllabus, with support through the use of cooperative learning and a continued focus on fluency and comprehension.

A typical Strategic Reading daily lesson incorporates four complementary learning activities:

> (1) The reading showcase: the teacher models the comprehension strategies of a mature reader, by "reading aloud and thinking aloud" to the class, commenting on what's going through her mind as she mentally interacts with the author. (2) The mini-lesson: the teacher instructs the class in a specific strategy (such as skimming subheadings and captions before reading an informational text), in elements of the writer's craft (such as the use of symbolism in literature), in word patterns in the context of reading (such as prefixes and suffixes), and in social skills for working in cooperative teams discussing reading. (3) Student team literature: students work in pairs or small teams to read together selected high-interest novels, poetry, and plays, and to discuss comprehension questions provided in guides. (4) Self-selected reading and writing centers: each student can choose items to read independently, do various writing activities, or listen to an audiotape accompanying a book (Partnership for Reading 2002, online).

A strength of the program is the professional development and support provided for teachers. Each teacher attends a three-day workshop, with participants role-playing the role of student and then of teacher. In addition, expert in-class peer coaches are available as teachers become comfortable with using the new system.

Schoolwide Support for High School Struggling Readers

Clearly, adequately addressing struggling readers' needs in high school requires a multi-faceted approach: specialized reading instruction, classroom teachers who understand and are capable of teaching reading and study strategies appropriate to content areas, and special study supports such as tutoring.

The ultimate goal of reading instruction is to develop independent readers and thinkers. Reading is a tool that spans disciplines, is integrated into all content areas, and addresses delivery. A reading program is not a reading class; it is a total school's commitment to literacy (High School Reading Task Force of the Madison Metropolitan School District 1999, online).

The High School Reading Task Force of the Madison Metropolitan School District (Wisc.) recommends the following roles for school-based personnel in support for struggling readers at the high school level:

The Principal:

- Understands what adolescent literacy is and what it requires

- Hires a reading specialist

- Schedules extra class time for struggling readers to receive instruction in addition to English or language arts, i.e. 90-minute block or an extra reading period

- Collaborates with reading personnel to develop a school reading profile including student data and available reading services

- Designs a system for heightening teacher awareness of both the reading profile and the strategies/resources to meet the needs of students

- Assigns reading staff for the reading program, including additional instruction for struggling readers

- Evaluates the school reading program

- Provides leadership and demonstrates ongoing support for a school-wide reading program

- Acknowledges the importance of implementing reading strategies across the curriculum

- Promotes and celebrates literacy events school-wide, i.e. book fairs, reading incentives, etc.

- Supports a total school sustained silent-reading time each day

Classroom Teacher Level:

- Understands that reading is a process of learning to gain meaning from print

- Models reading for pleasure as well as for content

- Reads aloud to students for various purposes, i.e., to demonstrate the thinking process, to share the sheer joy of reading

- Provides pre-reading, during reading and post-reading activities

- Is aware of and implements reading and writing strategies across the curriculum

- Works with the reading specialist to meet individual student needs

- Monitors reading progress of students

- Provides time for students to practice and enjoy reading

- Provides a variety of reading experiences (lab, text, newspapers, current events materials), some student self-selected

- Consciously and consistently implements the goals of the school-wide reading program (1999, online).

The Alliance for Excellent Education developed case studies in support of its publication *Every Child a Graduate: A Framework for an Excellent Education for All Middle and High School Students*, which was issued in 2002. Two of these are provided below. The report and additional case studies can be accessed at http://www.all4ed.org/publications/.

Sarasota, Fla.—Meeting the Secondary Reading Challenge: Interdisciplinary Reading in the Content Areas

The Sarasota County Public School District dedicates a section of its Web site to Meeting the Secondary Reading Challenge: Interdisciplinary Reading in the Content Areas. This site provides several reading strategies that assist teachers in incorporating literacy into the instruction of all subjects. Strategies include vocabulary building, graphic organizers, journals, note-taking, and activities for before and after reading. One specific strategy is called "photographed vocabulary," which helps students retain more information because the vocabulary word is experienced or visualized. For instance, a student will better remember and understand the meaning of the word "timid" if he or she acts out the word in front of the classroom. Another strategy is to use Venn Diagrams, which can help to compare and contrast characters, systems, operations, or attributes. Overall, there are over 30 different reading strategies to help students succeed in all subject areas.

The Web site also includes training information and strategies of the Creating Independence through Student-owned Strategies (CRISS) Project, which is designed to develop thoughtful and independent learners by enabling them to be in charge of their own learning. CRISS strategies help students to better organize, understand, and retain course information. To enhance student learning, CRISS employs the following concepts:

- Students must be able to integrate new information with prior knowledge.

- Students need to be actively involved in their own learning by discussing, writing, and organizing.

- Students must self-monitor to identify which strategies are the most effective for a given learning task (retrieved from http://www.all4ed.org/publications/Sarasota.html).

Denver, Colo.—Reading and Writing Studio Course

In August 2002, hundreds of Denver's middle-and high-school students ended their summer vacations with a surprise waiting for them. They returned to school to find that their schedules included the Reading and Writing Studio Course, a part of the district's new focus on literacy. The two-period-per-day program focuses on students reading below grade level and requires them to read a million words a year (about 25 adult-length books) and to write everyday. The program recruits, hires, and trains literacy coaches who provide detailed lesson plans that describe mini-lessons and then give students the opportunity to read, write, and work on skills such as using quotation marks. Literacy coaches also work with other teachers to ensure that the studies are taught effectively and that lessons are reinforced in other classes.

The program also calls for eight area literacy specialists, two for each quadrant, who oversee the literacy coaches. The literacy coaches, specialists, teachers and principals are required to attend a 10-day summer training institute as well as other professional development and training institutes periodically throughout the school year. Literacy coaches receive a $5,000 stipend separate from their salaries, using Title I funds. To date, over $8 million dollars of federal Title I funds have been used towards this literacy program. In addition, libraries connected to the program have received private funding to buy books and create a new library for the students (retrieved from http://www.all4ed.org/publications/Denver.html).

Professional Development

Given the pressure to meet state and national standards, as well as the increasing numbers of students with limited English proficiency and students with disabilities in general education classrooms, middle and high school teachers are now more than ever before in need of training that will help them enhance learning for all students, particularly those who struggle with reading. Greenleaf, Jimenez, and Roller (2002) size up the situation plainly:

> ...[T]o a large degree, whether or not ongoing reading instruction, and at what quality, is offered to students depends on ongoing and high-quality professional development opportunities for classroom teachers to develop knowledge about reading in their subject areas (490).

There are two areas in which content-area teachers need to be proficient: understanding what strategic reading is, and how to incorporate effective reading strategies into their curriculum (Barton 1997). Support for middle and high school teachers should include:

- reading specialist services, including resource support and current research on literacy and learning;

- training in instructional strategies, including discussion of theory, modeling, coaching, and practice;

- time for collaborative planning with other teachers; and

- ongoing support groups that focus on problem sharing and resolution with their colleagues as well as incorporating participation by a group facilitator (Barton 1997; Raiche and Showers 2000; Vacca 2002; Vaughn, Klinger, and Bryant 2001).

Reading specialists play a particularly critical role. Henwood (2000) writes that the reading specialist is most effective when she is part of a collaborative culture, in which her role is to provide tangible support, offer recognition and appreciation of teachers' efforts to change, involve colleagues in decision making, and refer to knowledge bases and not to personal style when collaborating. Issues with which the classroom teacher might want help from the reading specialist include:

- individualizing help and dealing with a large class size;

- handling comprehension/decoding problems;

- including special needs learners;

- improving notetaking skills;

- teaching to multiple reading levels;

- training high school reading tutors;

- using the textbook more effectively;

- giving suggestions to parents for helping children with reading;

- getting supplemental materials; and

- helping students with research projects (Henwood 2000).

The teachers with whom Henwood worked cited the following benefits of collaborating with the reading specialist: it led to positive changes in pedagogy; it forced the teachers to reflect on their practice; and it allowed the teachers to experience learning individualized to their needs. For the students, the benefits included receiving feedback from more than one person and having a chance to work with different teaching styles.

A promising practice being used in an increasing number of schools and school districts is the provision of "literacy coaches." These people typically are selected for their expertise in the teaching of reading and their ability to teach adults—specifically, the teachers in each school. Literacy coaches might help to develop professional development for teachers and also provide a link across departments in an effort to encourage a schoolwide focus on the literacy needs of adolescents. Most importantly, though, they provide ongoing help to teachers by meeting with teacher teams to analyze data and plan instructional strategies, teach model lessons, and work one-on-one with teachers who are working to develop a broader repertoire of approaches to help struggling readers increase their skill levels (Sturtevant 2003).

With targeted professional development opportunities, middle and high school teachers who were previously unfamiliar with reading instruction can quickly develop their expertise. Collaboration (with the reading specialist or other content-area teachers) is a critical tool that enables teachers to hone their understanding of reading processes and their practice of strategy instruction.

The Role of the Principal

New literacy initiatives demand strong leadership, vision, and support. Here are some ways principals can maximize the effectiveness of such programs:

- *Be open to something different.* New programs may involve changes in classroom spaces, activity level, and noise.

- *Help teachers make the transition.* Aid them in recognizing the difficulties, and applaud their successes.

- *Know the audience.* Work with teachers to identify what types of readers could benefit from a program.

- *Be a source of stability.* Make sure courses for struggling readers are not populated just by transient students, and do not allow students to transfer into the course after the first few weeks of school.

- *Make it important.* Make special literacy programs a scheduling priority, and select a highly regarded teacher to lead teacher development and discussions about the teaching of reading.

- *Take an active part.* Visit the classrooms that are implementing the program on a regular basis and talk with students about what they are learning (Codding 2001).

Section Nine

Conclusion

Reading is not simply an isolated subject that is mastered in elementary school and then never in need of being taught again. On the contrary, reading—and literacy in general—is a critical tool that must continue to be developed in adolescence and beyond. The goal of adolescent literacy is well-stated by the Rand Reading Study Group:

> The proficient adult reader can read a variety of materials with ease and interest, can read for varying purposes, and can read with comprehension even when the material is neither easy to understand nor intrinsically interesting (2002, xiii).

Our reading abilities are fundamentally tied to other important life skills, such as communicating thoughts through writing, discussing and analyzing information with others, gaining knowledge, improving vocabulary, and following written directions. Furthermore, reading for pleasure is often an end in itself. Getting absorbed in good books allows individuals to develop their personal interests, take time out from hectic activities, and engage in a creative solitary activity—which can contribute to a greater sense of balance amid life's pastimes and pursuits.

In many ways, adolescence is an opportune time to enhance reading and thinking skills. Middle and high school students are at a stage in life in which they are developing cognitive abilities that allow them to grapple with more complex ideas. They are also dealing with important issues involving identity, relations with others, and planning for their futures as adults. Educators can take advantage of these unique circumstances when developing reading instruction. For example, they can both challenge and strengthen students' emerging thinking abilities by using techniques such as student debates, thematic units, and small-group discussion.

In order to successfully develop reading skills, readers must be active. Active readers are engaged with the text; they search for meaning; they are aware of their purposes for reading; they are interested in what they are learning; and they connect what they are reading with their prior knowledge or their own personal experiences. Research findings underscore the importance of promoting active reading. Some elements of instruction found to be effective include: small-group discussions about reading materials, activating background knowledge before reading, instruction in comprehension strategies such as monitoring comprehension, opportunities to respond to reading by writing in dialogue journals, interactive types of computer-assisted reading activities, and choice in reading materials.

A number of studies have found interactive approaches to be highly beneficial for low-achieving secondary students. At the same time, though, these and other students need support to develop component skills in order to become independent readers. Research findings in this area are encouraging, indicating strategic reading skills can be taught and textbook adaptations are effective in increasing understanding of the material.

The issue of assessment must be carefully considered. The recent literature on assessment has emphasized the importance of matching the test to the task: if reading is an active process, assessment of reading comprehension should also be active. Whereas short-answer and standardized tests have a place in the curriculum, more emphasis should be placed on forms of assessment that promote learning as a meaning-making process. Assessment should be treated as a part of the learning process, not as an entirely separate activity.

Finally, a number of suggestions have been provided to secondary school educators—both English teachers and other content-area teachers—for integrating reading instruction into the curriculum. When reading instruction and reading-related activities are incorporated into the curriculum rather than simply appended to it, the goal of improving reading skills becomes time-efficient. Moreover, this approach has the potential to draw attention to reading as a meaningful and enjoyable activity, and it serves as a demonstration of the central role literacy plays in the many and varied tasks of our lives.

References

Alfassi, M. (1998). Reading for meaning: The efficacy of reciprocal teaching in fostering reading comprehension in high school students in remedial reading classes. *American Educational Research Journal, 35*(2), 309-332.

Alliance for Excellent Education. (2003). Alliance letter to President Bush. Retrieved from http://www.all4ed.org/whats_at_stake/PresidentLetter.html

Allington, R.L. (2002). You can't learn much from books you can't read. *Educational Leadership, 60*(3),16-19.

Alvermann, D.E., et al. (1996). Middle and high school students' perceptions of how they experience text-based discussions: A multicase study. *Reading Research Quarterly* (July-September 1996), 244-267.

Applebee, A.N. (1993). *Literature in the Secondary School: Studies of Curriculum and Instruction in the United States.* Urbana, IL: National Council of Teachers of English.

Association for Supervision and Curriculum Development. (2000). Before it's too late: Giving reading a last chance. *ASCD Curriculum Update,* Summer.

Atwell, N. (1998). *In the Middle: Writing, Reading, and Learning with Adolescents (second edition).* Portsmouth, NH: Heinemann.

Barry, A.L. (2002). Reading strategies teachers say they use. *Journal of Adolescent & Adult Literacy, 46*(2),132-141.

Barton, M.L. (1997). Addressing the literacy crisis: Teaching reading in the content areas. *NASSP Bulletin* (March, 1997), 22-30.

Beck, I.L., and McKeown, M.G. (2002). Questioning the author: Making sense of social studies. *Educational Leadership, 60*(3), 44-47.

Bernhardt, B. (1994). Reading and writing between the lines: An interactive approach using computers. *Journal of Reading, 37*(6), 458-463.

Bonds, C.W., Bonds, L.G. and Peach, W. (1992). Metacognition: Developing independence in learning. *The Clearing House, 66* (1), 56-59.

Broadus, K. and Ivey, G. (2002). Taking away the struggle to read in the middle grades. *Middle School Journal* (November 2002), 5-11.

Brozo, W.G. (1990). Learning how at-risk readers learn best: A case for interactive assessment. *Journal of Reading, 33*(7), 522-527.

Brozo, W.G., and Hargis, C. (2003). Taking seriously the idea of reform: One high school's efforts to make reading more responsive to all students. *Journal of Adolescent and Adult Literacy, 47*(1), 14-23.

Brucker, P.O., and Piazza, R. (2002). Reading instruction for older students. *CEC Today* (September/October 2002), 12-13.

Burke, J. (2002). The Internet reader. *Educational Leadership, 60*(3), 38-42.

Burroughs, R. (1993). Supporting successful literature programs: Lessons from a new national survey. *School Library Media Quarterly, 21*(3), 159-163.

Call, P.E. (1991). SQ3R + what I know sheet = one strong strategy (open to suggestion). *Journal of Reading, 35*(1), 50-52.

Casteel, C.P., Isom, B.A., and Jordan, K.F. (2000). Creating confident and competent readers: Transactional strategies instruction. *Intervention in School and Clinic* (November 2000), 67-74.

Chan, L.K.S. (1994). Relationship of motivation, strategic learning, and reading achievement in grades 5, 7, and 9. *Journal of Experimental Education, 62*(4), 319-339.

Cheek, E.H., Jr. (1992). Selecting appropriate informal reading assessment procedures. *Middle School Journal, 24*(1), 33-36.

Ciborowski, J. (1992). *Textbooks and the students who can't read them: A guide to teaching content.* Boston: Brookline Books.

Cochran, J.A. (1993). *Reading in the content areas for junior high and high school.* Boston: Allyn and Bacon.

Codding, J. (2001). An up ramp for struggling readers. *Principal Leadership* (October), 22-25.

Collins, N.D. (1996). *Motivating low-performing adolescent readers.* Bloomington, IN: ERIC Clearinghouse on Reading, English, and Communication. Retrieved from http://www.ericfacility.net/databases/ERIC_Digests/ed396265.html

Crooks, T.J. (1988). The impact of classroom evaluation practices on students. *Review of Educational Research, 58*(4), 438-481.

Crowley, M.L. (1993). Student mathematics portfolio: More than a display case. *The Mathematics Teacher, 86*(7), 544-547.

Curran, C.E. (1997). Analyzing story characters: Facilitating higher level comprehension skills in students with learning disabilities. *Intervention in School and Clinic* (May 1997), 312-315.

Curtis, M.E. (2002). *Adolescent reading: A synthesis of research. Paper presented at Workshop II: Practice models for adolescent literacy success.* Baltimore: U.S. Department of Education, Office of Vocational and Adult Education. Retrieved from http://216.26.160.105/conf/nichd/synthesis.asp

D'Arcangelo, M. (2002). The challenge of content-area reading: A conversation with Donna Ogle. *Educational Leadership, 60*(3), 12-15.

Davidson, J. and Koppenhaver, D. (1993). *Adolescent literacy: What works and why.* New York: Garland Publishing, Inc.

DeGroff, L. (1990). Is there a place for computers in whole language classrooms? *The Reading Teacher, 33*(7), 568-572.

Divine, K.P. and Whanger, R.E. (1990). Use of a computer learning laboratory with at-risk high school students. *Educational Technology, 30*(6), 46-48.

Ecroyd, C.A. (1991). Motivating students through reading aloud. *English Journal, 80*(6), 76-78.

Educational Alliance at Brown University. (2003). Teen literacy across the curriculum. Retrieved from http://www.alliance.brown.edu/stories/story0103.shtml

Educational Alliance at Brown University. (n.d.). *Adolescent Literacy in the Content Areas.* Retrieved from http://www.knowledgeloom.org/adlit/index.jsp

Flanagan, B. (1996). *Improving students' understanding of textbook content.* Retrieved from http://www.ldonline.org/ ld_indepth/teaching_techniques/understanding_textbooks.html

Foil, C.R., and Alber, S.R. (2002). Fun and effective ways to build your students' vocabulary. *Intervention in School and Clinic* (January 2002), 131-139.

Fuchs, L.S., Fuchs, D., and Kazdan, S. (1999). Effects of peer-assisted learning strategies on high school students with serious reading problems. *Remedial and Special Education, 20*(5), 309-318.

Fuentes, P. (1998). Reading comprehension in mathematics. *The Clearing House, 72*(2), 81-88.

Fuhler, C.J. (1994). Response journals: Just one more time with feeling. *Journal of Reading, 37*(5), 400-405.

Gauthier, L.R. (1989). Understanding content material (in the classroom). *Reading Teacher, 43*(3), 266-267.

Gentile, L.M., and McMillan, M.M. (1994). Critical dialogue: The road to literacy for students at risk in middle schools. *Middle School Journal, 25*(4), 50-54.

Goodman, K.S. (1992). Whole language research: Foundations and development. In *What research has to say about reading instruction.* Second edition. Ed. S. Jay Samuels and Alan E. Farstrup, pp. 46-69. Newark, DE: International Reading Association.

Green, M. (1998). Rapid retrieval of information: Reading aloud with a purpose. *Journal of Adolescent and Adult Literacy* (December-January 1997-1998), 306-307.

Greene, J.F. (1998). Another chance: Help for older students with limited literacy. *American Educator* (Spring/Summer), 74-79.

Greenleaf, C.L., Jimenez, R.T., and Roller, C.M. (2002). Reclaiming secondary reading interventions: From limited to rich conceptions, from narrow to broad conversations. *Reading Research Quarterly, 37*(4), 484-496.

Greenwood, S.C. (2002). Making words matter: Vocabulary study in the content areas. *The Clearing House, 75*(5), 258-263.

Gross, P.A. (1991). Interactive reading on the secondary level. Paper presented at the Annual Meeting of the National Reading Conference (41st, Palm Springs, CA, December 3-7, 1991). ERIC Document Number 359 490.

Gross, P.A. (1992). Shared meaning: Whole language reader response at the secondary level. Paper presented at the Annual Meeting of the National Reading Conference (42nd, San Antonio, TX, December 2-5, 1992). ERIC Document No. 359 491.

Guthrie, J.T., Anderson, E., Alao, S., and Rinehart, J. (1999). Influences of concept-oriented reading instruction on strategy use and conceptual learning from text. *Elementary School Journal* (March 1999), 343-366.

Guzzetti, B.J. (1990). Enhancing comprehension through trade books in high school English classes. *Journal of Reading, 33*(6), 411-413.

Haggard, M.R. (1986). The vocabulary self-collection strategy: Using student interest and world knowledge to enhance vocabulary growth. *Journal of Reading, 29*(7), 634-642.

Harmon, J.M. (2002). Teaching independent word learning strategies to struggling readers. *Journal of Adolescent & Adult Literacy, 45*(7), 606-615.

Helfeldt, J.P., and Henk, W.A. (1990). Reciprocal question-answer relationships: An instructional technique for at-risk readers. *Journal of Reading, 33*(7), 509-514.

Henwood, G.F. (2000). A new role for the reading specialist: Contributing toward a high school's collaborative educational culture. *Journal of Adolescent & Adult Literacy, 43*(4), 316-325.

Herman, P.A., Anderson, R.C., Pearson, D.P., and Nagy, W.E. (1987). Incidental acquisition of word meaning from expositions with varied text features. *Reading Research Quarterly, 22*(3), 263-284.

Hibbing, A.N., and Rankin-Erickson, J.L. (2003). A picture is worth a thousand words: Using visual images to improve comprehension for middle school struggling readers. *The Reading Teacher* (May 2003), 758-770.

Hickey, M.G. (1990). Reading and social studies: The critical connection. *Social Education, 33*(7), 175-176.

High School Reading Task Force of the Madison Metropolitan School District. (1999). *High school reading task force report.* Madison, WI: Author. Retrieved from http://www.madison.k12.wi.us/tnl/langarts/hsread.htm#commitment

Hirsch, E.D., Jr. (2003). Reading comprehension requires knowledge–of words and the world. *American Educator* (Spring), 10-29.

Holloway, J.H. (1999). Improving the reading skills of adolescents. *Educational Leadership* (October 1999), 80-81.

International Reading Association. (1990). A reading-writing connection in the content areas (secondary perspectives). *Journal of Reading, 33*(5), 376-378.

International Reading Association. (1999). Summary of adolescent literacy, a position statement for the commission on adolescent literacy of the International Reading Association. Retrieved from http://www.reading.org/positions/adol_lit.html

Ivey, G. (1999). A multicase study in the middle school: Complexities among young adolescent readers. *Reading Research Quarterly* (April, May, June 1999), 172-192.

Ivey, G. (2003). "The teacher makes it explainable" and other reasons to read aloud in the intermediate grades. *The Reading Teacher* (May 2003), 812-814.

Jenkins, J.R., and Jenkins, L.M. (1987). Making peer tutoring work. *Educational Leadership, 44*(6), 64-68.

Johannessen, L.R. (1994). Enhancing response to literature: A matter of changing old habits. *English Journal, 83*(7), 66-70.

Johnson, D.W., and Johnson, R.T. (1988). Critical thinking through structured controversy. *Educational Leadership, 45*(8), 58-64.

Kamil, M.L. (2003). *Adolescents and literacy: Reading for the 21st century*. Washington, DC: Alliance for Excellent Education.

Katims, DS., and Harmon, J.M. (2000). Strategic instruction in middle school social studies: Enhancing academic and literacy outcomes for at-risk students. *Intervention in School and Clinic, 35*(5), 280-289.

Kellerman, K.K. (1991). Students' rejection of teacher choice of free reading books. M.A. Thesis, Kean College. ERIC Document Number 329 949.

Kletzien, S.B. and Hushion, B.C. (1992). Reading workshop: Reading, writing, thinking. *Journal of Reading, 35*(6), 444-451.

Klingner, J.K, and Vaughn, S. (1998). Using collaborative strategic reading. *Teaching Exceptional Children* (July/August 1998), 32-37.

Knoeller, C.P. (1994). Negotiating interpretations of text: The role of student-led discussions in understanding literature. *Journal of Reading, 37*(7), 572-80.

Krashen, S. (1993). *The power of reading: Insights from the research*. Englewood, CO: Libraries Unlimited, Inc.

Krogness, M.M. (1995). *Just teach me, Mrs. K: Talking, reading, and writing with resistant adolescent learners*. Portsmouth, NH: Heinemann.

Langer, J.A. (1993). Approaches toward meaning in low-and high-rated readers. Report Series 2.20. Albany, NY: National Research Center on Literature Teaching and Learning. ERIC Document Number 361 650.

Lawrence, J.M.B. et al. (1993). Television in the English curriculum (The round table). *English Journal, 82*(6), 77-79.

Leal, D.J. (1992). The nature of talk about three types of text during peer group discussions. *Journal of Reading Behavior, 24*(4), 313-38.

Lebzelter, S., and Nowacek, E.J. (1999). Reading strategies for secondary students with mild disabilities. *Intervention in School and Clinic* (March 1999), 212-219.

Loranger, A.L. (1999). The challenge of content area literacy: A middle school case study. *The Clearing House, 72*(4), 239-243.

Lyon, G.R. (1998). Overview of reading and literacy research. In Patton, S., and Holmes, M. (Eds.), *The keys to literacy*. Washington, DC: Council for Basic Education.

MacGregor, M. (1990). Reading and writing in mathematics. In *Language and mathematics*. Ed. Bickmore-Brand, J., pp. 100-108. Portsmouth, NH: Heinemann.

McIntosh, M.E., and Bear, D. (1993). Directed reading-thinking activities to promote learning through reading in mathematics. *Clearing House* (September-October 1993), 40-44.

Mallow, J.V. (1991). Reading science. *Journal of Reading, 34*(5), 324-338.

Manzo, A.V. and Manzo, U.C. (1990). Note cue: A comprehension and participation training strategy. *Journal of Reading, 33*(8), 608-611.

Marshall, J.D. (1987). The effects of writing on students' understanding of literary texts. *Research in the Teaching of English, 21*(1), 30-63.

Matthews, C.E. (1987). Lap reading for teenagers. *Journal of Reading, 30*(5), 410-413.

McWhirter, A.M. (1990). Whole language in the middle school. *The Reading Teacher, 43*(8), 562-565.

Meltzer, J., and Okashige, S.E. (2001). First literacy, then learning. *Principal Leadership* (October 2001), 16-21.

Menke, D., and Davey. B. (1994). Teachers' views of textbooks and text reading instruction: Experience matters. *Journal of Reading, 37*(6), 464-470.

Miller, L.J., Kohler, F.W., Ezell, H., Hoel, K., and Strain, P.S. (1993). Winning with peer tutoring: A teacher's guide. *Preventing School Failure, 37*(3), 14-18.

Morrow, L.M., Tracey, D.H., and Maxwell, C.M., eds. (1995). *A survey of family literacy in the United States.* Newark, DE: International Reading Association.

Moscrip, L.F. (1991). How to start a successful paperback book program. *English Journal, 80*(6), 79-80.

National Assessment Governing Board, U.S. Department of Education. (2002). *Reading framework for the 2003 National Assessment of Educational Progress.* Washington, DC: Author. Retrieved from http://www.nagb.org/pubs/read_fw_03.pdf

National Assessment Governing Board, U.S. Department of Education. (2003). *Reading 2003: Major results.* Retrieved from http://nces.ed.gov/nationsreportcard/reading/results2003/

National Assessment Governing Board, U.S. Department of Education. (2003b). *The nation's report card: Reading 2002 (executive summary).* Retrieved from http://nces.ed.gov/nationsreportcard/pubs/main2002/2003521.asp#section2a

National Center for Education Statistics. (1996). *Reading proficiency and home support for literacy.* Washington, DC: U.S. Department of Education.

National Center for Education Statistics. (2001). *Outcomes of learning: Results from the 2000 program for international student assessment of 15-year-olds in reading, math, and science.* Washington, DC: U.S. Department of Education.

National Center for Education Statistics. (2001b). The nation's report card: Fourth-grade reading 2000. *Education Statistics Quarterly* (Summer 2001). Retrieved from http://nces.ed.gov/pubs2001/quarterly/summer/q2-1.asp

National Center for Education Statistics. (2001c). *National assessment of educational progress (NAEP), 1984 and 1999 long-term assessment.* Washington, DC: Author. Retrieved from http://nces.ed.gov/programs/coe/2001/charts/chart22.asp

National Commission on Writing in America's Schools and Colleges. (2003). *The neglected "R": The need for a writing revolution.* New York: The College Board.

National Reading Panel. (2000). Teaching *children to read: An evidence-based assessment of the scientific research literature on reading and its implications for reading instruction.* Washington, DC: National Institute of Child Health and Human Development.

Nystrand, M., Gamoran, A., and Heck, M.J. (1993). Using small groups for response to and thinking about literature. *English Journal 82,*(1), 14-22.

O'Sullivan, J.T. (1992). Reading beliefs and reading achievement: A development study of students from low income families. Report Number 6. *Summary reports of paths to literacy and illiteracy in Newfoundland and Labrador.* Newfoundland: Memorial University, St. Johns. ERIC Document Number 354 505.

Ostler, E. (1997). The effect of learning mathematical reading strategies on secondary students' homework grades. *Clearing House* (September-October 1997), 37-40.

Palincsar, A.S., & Herrenkohl, L.R. (2003). Designing collaborative learning contexts. *Theory into Practice, 41*(1), 26-32.

Partnership for Reading. (2002). *Summary of the second adolescent literacy workshop: Practice models for adolescent literacy success.* Retrieved from http://www.nifl.gov/partnershipforreading/adolescent/summaryIIa.html

Peak, J. and Dewalt, M.W. (1994). Reading achievement: Effects of computerized reading management and enrichment. *ERS Spectrum, 12*(1), 31-34.

Penney, C.G. (2002). Teaching decoding skills to poor readers in high school. *Journal of Literacy Research, 34*(1), 99-118.

Peresich, M.L., Meadows, J.D., and Sinatra. R. (1990). Content area cognitive mapping for reading and writing proficiency. *Journal of Reading, 33*(6), 424-432.

Peterson, C.L., Caverly, D.C., Nicholson, S.A., O'Neal, S., and Cusenbary, S. (2000). *Building reading proficiency at the secondary school level: A guide to resources.* Austin, TX: Southwest Educational Development Laboratory. Retrieved from http://www.sedl.org/pubs/catalog/items/read16.html

Podl, J.B. (1995). Introducing teens to the pleasures of reading. *Educational Leadership* (September 1995), 56-57.

Pottle, J.L. (1996). Using trade books to make connections across the curriculum. *Clearing House* (September-October 1996), 52-53.

Raiche, N., and Showers, B. (2000). A second chance to learn to read. *Leadership* (November/December 2000), 18-20.

Rand Reading Study Group. (2002). *Reading for understanding: Toward an R&D program in reading comprehension.* Santa Monica, CA: Rand Corporation.

Rekrut, M.D. (1994). Peer and cross-age tutoring: The lessons of research. *Journal of Reading, 37*(5), 356-362.

Riggs, E.G., and Gil-Garcia, A. (2001). *Helping middle and high school readers: Teaching and learning strategies across the curriculum.* Arlington, VA: Educational Research Service.

Roller, C.M. and Beed, P.L. (1994). Sometimes the conversations were grand, and sometimes ..." *Language Arts, 71*(7), 509-515.

Rosenshine, B., and Meister, C. (1994). Reciprocal teaching: A review of the research. *Review of Educational Research, 64*(4), 479-530.

Ruddell, M.R., and Shearer, B.A. (2002). "Extraordinary", "Tremendous," "Exhilarating," "Magnificent": Middle school at-risk students become avid word learners with the vocabulary self-collection strategy (VSS). *Journal of Adolescent & Adult Literacy, 45*(5), 352-363.

Salembier, G.B. (1999). SCAN and RUN: A reading comprehension strategy that works. *Journal of Adolescent and Adult Literacy* (February 1999), 386-394.

Salinger, T. (2003). Helping older, struggling readers. *Preventing School Failure, 47*(2), 79-85.

Schauer, D.K., and Beyersdorfer, J.M. (1992). Building active readers through debate (open to suggestion). *Journal of Reading, 36*(1), 57-58.

Schumm, J.S., and Mangrum II, C.T. (1991). FLIP: A framework for content area reading. *Journal of Reading, 35*(2),120-124.

Schumm, J.S., Vaughn, S, and Saumell. L. (1992). What teachers do when the textbook ts tough: Students speak out. *Journal of Reading Behavior, 24*(4), 481-502.

Scott, J.E. (1994). Literature circles in the middle school classroom: Developing reading, responding, and responsibility. *Middle School Journal, 26*(2), 37-41.

Sensenbaugh, R. (1990). Process writing in the classroom (ERIC/RCS). *Journal of Reading, 33*(5), 382-383.

Simic, M.R. (1993). *Guidelines for computer-assisted reading instruction (ERIC Digest).* Bloomington, IN: ERIC Clearinghouse on Reading and Communication Skills.

Singer, H. and Donlan, D. (1982). Active comprehension: Problem-solving schema with question generation for comprehension of complex short stories. *Reading Research Quarterly, 17*(2),168-186.

Sivin-Kachala, J., Bialo, E., and Rosso, J.L. (1998). *Online and electronic research by middle school students.* Santa Monica, CA: Milken Family Foundation.

Slavin, R. (1986). Learning together. *American Educator, 10*(2), 6-13.

Slater, W.H., and Horstman, F.R. (2002). Teaching reading and writing to struggling middle school and high School students: The case for reciprocal teaching. *Preventing School Failure, 46*(4), 163-166.

Smith, M.W. (1992). Effects of direct instruction on ninth graders' understanding of unreliable narrators. *Journal of Educational Research, 85*(6), 339-347.

Spiak, D.S. (1999). Reciprocal reading and main idea identification. *Teaching and Change, 6*(2), 212-219.

Spicer, J. (2003). Using picture books in high school math. *ENC Focus* (October 2003), 5.

Squire, J.R. (2004) Chapter 6a: Langauge arts. In G. Cawelti, (ed.), *Handbook of Research on Improving Student Achievement* (third edition), pp. 127-142. Arlington, VA: Educational Research Service.

Strong, R.W., Silver, H.F., Perini, M.J., and Tuculescu, G.M. (2002). *Reading for academic success: Powerful strategies for struggling, average, and advanced readers, grades 7-12.* Thousand Oaks, CA: Corwin Press, Inc.

Sturtevant, E.G. (2003). *The literacy coach: A key to improving teaching and learning in secondary schools*. Washington, DC: Alliance for Excellent Education.

Sullivan, A.M. (1988). The personal anthology: A stimulus for exploratory reading. *English Journal, 77*(1), 27-30.

Swanson, P.N., and De La Paz, S. (1998). Teaching effective comprehension strategies to students with learning and reading disabilities. *Intervention in School and Clinic* (March 1998), 209-218.

Sweigart, W. (1991). Classroom talk, knowledge development, and writing. *Research in the Teaching of English, 25*(4), 469-496.

Tanner, M.L., and Casados, L. (1998). Promoting and studying discussions in math classes. *Journal of Adolescent and Adult Literacy* (February 1998), 342-350.

Tuley, S.L. (1994). Creative testing: Hamlet, Celie, and Gulliver rendezvous in a final exam. *English Journal, 83*(8), 77-80.

Turner, J. (2003). Integrating writing into the content areas. *ERS Informed Educator Series*. Arlington, VA: Educational Research Service.

Vacca, R.T.(2002). Decoders to strategic readers. *Educational Leadership, 60*(3), 7-11.

Vacca, R.T., and Vacca, J.A.L. (1993). *Content area reading*. New York: Harper-Collins.

Vaughn, J.L. and Estes, T.H. (1986). *Reading and reasoning beyond the primary grades*. Boston: Allyn & Bacon.

Vaughn, S., Klinger, J.K., and Bryant, D.P. (2001). Collaborative strategic reading as a means to enhance peer-mediated instruction for reading comprehension and content-area learning. *Remedial and Special Education, 22*(2), 66-74.

Viadero, D. (1995). Even as popularity soars, portfolios encounter roadblocks. *Education Week* (April 5), 8-9.

Viau, E.A. (1998). Color me a writer: Teaching students to think critically. *Learning and Leading with Technology* (February 1998), 17-20.

Walberg, H.J., & Paik, S.J. (2004). Chapter 2: Effective general practices. In G. Cawelti, (ed.), *Handbook of Research on Improving Student Achievement* (third edition), pp. 25-38. Arlington, VA: Educational Research Service.

Weaver, C. (1994). *Reading process and practice: From socio-psycholinguistics to whole language*. Second Edition. Portsmouth, NH: Heinemann.

Weedman, D.L., and Weedman, M.C. (2001). When questions are the answers. *Principal Leadership* (October 2001), 42-46.

Wells, M.C. (1993). At the junction of reading and writing: How dialogue journals contribute to students' reading development. *Journal of Reading, 36*(4), 294-302.

Wepner, S.B. (1990). Computers, reading software, and at-risk eighth graders. *Journal of Reading, 34*(4), 264-268.

White, B. (1992). Preparing middle school students to respond to literature. *Middle School Journal, 24*(1), 21-23.

Whittier, P., and Blokker, B. (2001). Starting where they are. *Principal Leadership* (October), 52-55.

Wiencek, J. and O'Flahavan, J.F. (1994). From teacher-led to peer discussions about literature: Suggestions for making the shift. *Language Arts, 71*(7), 488-497.

Williams, M. (2001). Making connections: A workshop for adolescents who struggle with reading. *Journal of Adolescent & Adult Literacy, 44*(7), 588-602.

Wood, S.N. (2001). Bridging us the way to know: The novels of Gary Paulsen. *English Journal* (January 2001), 67-72.

Wood, K.D. (2002). Aiding comprehension with the imagine, elaborate, predict, and confirm (IEPC) strategy. *Middle School Journal* (January 2002), 47-54.

Worthy, J., Moorman, M., & Turner, M. (1999). What Johnny likes to read is hard to find in school. *Reading Research Quarterly* (January-March 1999), 12-27.

Wright, D.J. (1998). Choosing to read: Overcoming reading apathy. *Teaching and Change, 5*(3-4), 225-231.

Index

I

Imagine, Elaborate, Predict, and Confirm 57

independent reading 29, 44, 40, 71, 94

informal reading inventories 75, 77

INSERT 59

International Reading Association 7, 11, 41

Internet 7, 46, 63

inventories 20, 75, 77

Isom 55

IT FITS 62

Ivey 25, 27, 30, 32, 44

J

Jenkins 65

Jimenez 13, 15, 100

Johnson 42

Jordan 55

journal 6, 14, 20, 38, 39, 41, 71, 72, 84

journals 17, 23, 29, 39, 40, 41, 70, 98, 104

K

Kamil 45, 47

Katims 81

Klesch-Kincaid Reading Level 88

Kletzien 14, 24

Klinger 13, 37, 100

Koppenhaver 18

Krashen 26, 28, 30

Krogness 18, 20

KWL 52

L

LANGUAGE! 15

Leal 33

libraries 21, 25, 26, 99, 117

library 25, 26, 28, 29, 32, 45, 63, 99, 117

literacy coaches 99, 101

literature 13, 14, 15, 18, 23, 24, 26, 27, 28, 31, 33, 35, 36, 42, 46, 70, 71, 73, 79, 85, 89, 94, 95, 104

Literature Immersion 13

literature-based 14, 15

M

Madison Metropolitan School District 96

magazine 90

magazines 7, 25, 81

Mallow 82

Manzo 36

Marshall 72

McIntosh 57

McMillan 36

McWhirter 24

Meadows 58

meaning-making 69, 71, 104

Meister 53

Miller 65

miscue analysis 75, 77

modeling 20, 29, 36, 54, 56, 57, 58, 65, 67, 72, 100

Moorman 25

motivation 10, 12, 14, 20, 28, 44, 68, 70, 76, 77, 84, 88, 91, 93

ORDER FORM FOR RELATED RESOURCES

Quantity	Item # and Title	Base Price	ERS Individual Subscriber Discount Price	ERS School District Subscriber Discount Price	Total Price
			Price Per Item		
	What We Know About: Reading at the Middle and High School Levels, Third Edition (#0536)	$20	$15	$10	
	What We Know About: Helping Middle and High School Readers (#0448)	$18	$13.50	$9	
	What We Know About: Effective Early Reading Instruction (#0449)	$20	$15	$10	
	Handbook of Research on Improving Student Achievement (#0538)	$44	$33	$22	

Postage and Handling ** (Add the greater of $4.50 or 10% of purchase price.):	
Express Delivery ** (Add $20 for second-business-day service.):	
TOTAL DUE:	

** Please double for international orders.

SATISFACTION GUARANTEED!

If you are not satisfied with an ERS resource, return it in its original condition within 30 days of receipt and we will give you a full refund.

Method of payment:

☐ Check enclosed (payable to Educational Research Service).

☐ Purchase order enclosed. (P.O.#_____)

Bill my: ☐ VISA   ☐ MasterCard   ☐ American Express

Name on Card (print) _____

Account Number _____   Expiration Date _____

Signature _____   Date _____

Visit us online at www.ers.org for a complete listing of resources!

Shipping address:

☐ Dr. ☐ Mr. ☐ Mrs. ☐ Ms.   Name _____

Position _____   ERS Subscriber ID# _____

School District or Agency _____

Street Address _____

City _____   State _____   Zip _____

Phone _____   Fax _____   Email _____

Return completed order form to: Educational Research Service
1001 North Fairfax Street, Suite 500, Alexandria, VA 22314
Phone: (800) 791-9308 • Fax: (800) 791-9309 • Email: ers@ers.org • Web site: www.ers.org

SUBSCRIPTIONS AT A GLANCE

If you are looking for reliable K-12 research to . . .

- *tackle the challenges of NCLB;*
- *identify research-based teaching practices;*
- *make educationally sound and cost-effective decisions; and most importantly*
- *improve student achievement . . .*

then you need look no further than an ERS Subscription.

Simply pick the subscription option that best meets your needs:

✓ **School District Subscription**—a special research and information subscription that provides education leaders with timely research on priority issues in K-12 education. All new ERS publications and periodicals, access to customized information services through the ERS special library, and 50 percent discounts on additional ERS resources are included in this subscription for one annual fee. This subscription also provides the entire administrative staff "instant" online, searchable access to the wide variety of ERS resources. You'll gain access to the ERS electronic library of more than 1,600 educational research-based documents, as well as additional content uploaded throughout the year.

✓ **Individual Subscription**—designed primarily for school administrators, staff, and school board members who want to receive a personal copy of new ERS studies, reports, and/or periodicals published and special discounts on other resources purchased.

✓ **Other Education Agency Subscription**—available for state associations, libraries, departments of education, service centers, and other organizations needing access to quality research and information resources and services.

Your ERS Subscription benefits begin as soon as your order is received and continue for 12 months. For more detailed subscription information and pricing, contact ERS toll free at (800) 791-9308, by email at ers@ers.org, or visit us online at www.ers.org!

Notes:

Notes: